Red Hat Certified Engineer (RHCE) Ansible Automation Study Guide

In-Depth Guidance and Practice

Alex Soto Bueno and Andrew Block

O'REILLY®

Red Hat Certified Engineer (RHCE) Ansible Automation Study Guide
by Alex Soto Bueno and Andrew Block

Printed in the United States of America.

Published by O'Reilly Media, Inc., 1005 Gravenstein Highway North, Sebastopol, CA 95472.

O'Reilly books may be purchased for educational, business, or sales promotional use. Online editions are also available for most titles (*http://oreilly.com*). For more information, contact our corporate/institutional sales department: 800-998-9938 or *corporate@oreilly.com*.

Acquisitions Editor: John Devins
Development Editor: Jeff Bleiel
Production Editor: Katherine Tozer
Copyeditor: Sonia Saruba
Proofreader: Andrea Schein
Indexer: Ellen Troutman-Zaig
Interior Designer: David Futato
Cover Designer: José Marzan Jr.
Illustrator: Kate Dullea

June 2025: First Edition

Revision History for the First Edition
2025-05-27: First Release

See *http://oreilly.com/catalog/errata.csp?isbn=9781098162139* for release details.

This work is part of a collaboration between O'Reilly and Red Hat Developer. See our statement of editorial independence (*https://oreil.ly/editorial-independence*).

978-1-098-16213-9

[LSI]

[Ada i Alexandra] Amor verdadero nos une por siempre en el latido de mi corazon.

—Alex

To all the engineers out there. Automate the planet!

—Andrew

Table of Contents

Preface

The Red Hat Certified Engineer (RHCE) exam focuses on the use of Ansible as a tool for managing the entire IT landscape. Like all Red Hat exams, it is completely performance based, and as such, requires a deep understanding of Ansible concepts, under time constraints. This book is designed to introduce you to the key areas of Ansible and walk you through the topics covered in the exam using practical and reliable examples so that you are adequately prepared.

Who Should Read This Book

This book is written for users interested in learning how to manage their infrastructure and systems with Ansible. Since automation plays an increasingly important role in the operation of infrastructure and applications, this book is of interest to a range of personas: everyone from system administrators seeking their next certification, to junior engineers looking to master new technologies and concepts, to software architects looking to stay on top of technology trends.

Users familiar with IT automation, the tools, and available common approaches will also see how Ansible is uniquely positioned to excel regardless of where it operates—on premises, in the cloud, or at the edge.

Why We Wrote This Book

Writing a book about Ansible was a natural step for us.

We started our careers as developers, and as we grew professionally, we started getting experience in the whole lifecycle of an application, from development to production. Over the years, we've seen firsthand how Ansible simplifies the complexities of automating IT processes, from system configuration to application deployment. Our experience with Ansible has made it clear that it's one of the most powerful, yet accessible, automation tools available.

We've seen this in our day-to-day work and with all customers who adopt this technology to operate their applications. This inspired us to create a comprehensive guide that would help others leverage Ansible to its fullest potential. Moreover, we've seen in the field how valuable becoming an Ansible-certified engineer is and how this boosts engineer careers. For this reason, we decided to write this book so you can level up your knowledge and career in Ansible.

Navigating This Book

Here is an overview of what we cover in the book:

- Chapter 1 gives an overview of the topics covered in the exam and discusses the benefits of certification.
- Chapter 2 provides an introduction to Ansible, including basic concepts, and lays the groundwork for the rest of the book.
- Chapter 3 introduces Ansible Playbooks, and walks through how to run your first playbook.
- Chapter 4 focuses on how Ansible manages hosts and how to organize and target automation against them.
- Chapter 5 looks at flow control and examines how to influence the execution of automation activities.
- Chapter 6 looks at how to manipulate files in Ansible, including basic operations and templating.
- Chapter 7 is a deep dive into Ansible modules and how to develop a new module.
- Chapter 8 covers how to organize Ansible content using roles and collections, their purpose, and how they enable you to package and share Ansible content with others.
- Chapter 9 introduces Ansible Execution Environments as a method for running Ansible automation, the challenges they solve, and how they can be created.
- Chapter 10 covers how to effectively manage systems using Ansible, and looks at management-related activities, including filesystem management and security considerations.

Conventions Used in This Book

The following typographical conventions are used in this book:

Italic
: Indicates new terms, URLs, email addresses, filenames, and file extensions.

`Constant width`
: Used for program listings, as well as within paragraphs to refer to program elements such as variable or function names, databases, data types, environment variables, statements, and keywords.

`Constant width bold`
: Shows commands or other text that should be typed literally by the user.

`Constant width italic`
: Shows text that should be replaced with user-supplied values or by values determined by context.

This element signifies a general note.

This element signifies a tip or suggestion.

This element signifies a warning.

This element signifies important information.

Using Code Examples

Supplemental material (code examples, exercises, etc.) is available for download at *https://github.com/lordofthejars/red-hat-certified-engineer-ansible-automation-study-guide-src*.

If you have a technical question or a problem using the code examples, please email *support@oreilly.com*.

This book is here to help you get your job done. In general, if example code is offered with this book, you may use it in your programs and documentation. You do not need to contact us for permission unless you're reproducing a significant portion of the code. For example, writing a program that uses several chunks of code from this book does not require permission. Selling or distributing examples from O'Reilly books does require permission. Answering a question by citing this book and quoting example code does not require permission. Incorporating a significant amount of example code from this book into your product's documentation does require permission.

We appreciate, but generally do not require, attribution. An attribution usually includes the title, author, publisher, and ISBN. For example: "*Red Hat Certified Engineer (RHCE) Ansible Automation Study Guide* by Alex Soto Bueno and Andrew Block (O'Reilly). Copyright 2025 Alex Soto Bueno and Andrew Block, 978-1-098-16213-9."

If you feel your use of code examples falls outside fair use or the permission given above, feel free to contact us at *permissions@oreilly.com*.

O'Reilly Online Learning

For more than 40 years, *O'Reilly Media* has provided technology and business training, knowledge, and insight to help companies succeed.

Our unique network of experts and innovators share their knowledge and expertise through books, articles, and our online learning platform. O'Reilly's online learning platform gives you on-demand access to live training courses, in-depth learning paths, interactive coding environments, and a vast collection of text and video from O'Reilly and 200+ other publishers. For more information, visit *https://oreilly.com*.

How to Contact Us

Please address comments and questions concerning this book to the publisher:

O'Reilly Media, Inc.
1005 Gravenstein Highway North
Sebastopol, CA 95472
800-889-8969 (in the United States or Canada)
707-827-7019 (international or local)
707-829-0104 (fax)
support@oreilly.com
https://oreilly.com/about/contact.html

We have a web page for this book, where we list errata, examples, and any additional information. You can access this page at *https://oreil.ly/red-hat-certified*.

For news and information about our books and courses, visit *https://oreilly.com*.

Find us on LinkedIn: *https://linkedin.com/company/oreilly-media*.

Watch us on YouTube: *https://youtube.com/oreillymedia*.

Acknowledgments

We would like to say thank you very much to our O'Reilly editor Jeff Bleiel, acquisitions editor John Devins, and production editor Katie Tozer, for your trust and supporting us.

Also thank you very much to the book's technical reviewers: Jan-Piet Mens, Marek Vette, and Raju Gandhi, because you help us make this book look perfect.

Alex Soto

Bit by bit, you'll end up finishing the book, but as in the movies, first the credits. I'd like to acknowledge Santa (yellow planes are better than yellow submarines), Uri (water at 2C works better, trust me), Guiri (2026 surt el Tour de Barcelona, yo aquí lo dejo), Gavina and Gabi (thanks for the support), and all my friends at the Red Hat developers team (we are the best).

Thank you to Jonathan Vila, Abel Salgado, and Jordi Sola for the fantastic conversations about Java and Kubernetes.

Last but certainly not least, I'd like to acknowledge Anita, "you fill up my senses...like a storm in the desert"; my parents Mili and Ramon for buying my first computer; my daughters Ada and Alexandra, "sou les ninetes dels meus ulls."

Andrew Block

Collaboration and shared experiences are what make writing technical publications possible. I would like to thank my fellow colleagues at Red Hat for their knowledge, experience, and guidance with Ansible automation over the years. In particular, a huge shout out to Chad Ferman who helped develop and deliver Ansible-based enablement hackathons worldwide, which help others see the possibilities that can be achieved through automation.

To the Red Hat Certification team members who provided guidance and helped shape what this publication would become.

And finally, I would like to thank my mother, who inspired me to realize my true potential—no matter how long (and painful) the journey was.

CHAPTER 1

Exam Details and Resources

If you have this book in your hands (literally or figuratively), it indicates that you are planning to use (or already using) Ansible.

This book is targeted at those who aspire to become a Red Hat Certified Engineer (RHCE), and in particular, those who are preparing for the Ansible EX294 (Red Hat Certified Engineer) exam.

The ultimate goal is to learn about Ansible, how to use it, and how it can be used to automate your day-to-day tasks as a system administrator.

Why Should You Be Certified?

Ansible is one of the most used DevOps tools in enterprises to automate the provisioning, configuration, and management of distributed and on-premises systems. Gartner evaluated Red Hat's DevOps solution (where Ansible is placed) in the new Magic Quadrant, recognizing it as a key tool for managing infrastructures.

If you are an IT professional, system administrator, or DevOps engineer, you are interested in becoming certified for the following reasons:

- It shows that you deeply understand Ansible and can apply it effectively in real-world scenarios.
- Because of the wide usage of Ansible in the industry, certification increases your career opportunities and distinguishes you from other candidates.
- It accelerates your career progression because certified professionals are often considered for senior roles.
- It boosts your skills in Ansible, making you more performant.

Ansible certification isn't just a credential that you acquire. It's an investment in your future. It will give you the skills to manage complex IT environments, help you stay ahead in the competitive job market, and position you as a trusted professional in automation and DevOps.

EX294 Prerequisites

Several prerequisites must be satisfied prior to beginning your certification journey:

- You must have earned the Red Hat Certified System Administrator (RHCSA) certification.
- You must have taken the Red Hat System Administration I (RH124), the Red Hat System Administration II (RH134), and the RHCSA Rapid Track Course (RH199). Or you must have comparable work experience as a system administrator on Red Hat Enterprise Linux.
- You must have taken Red Hat Enterprise: Linux Automation with Ansible (RH294) or have comparable work experience.

Let's start with the topics that will be covered in this book and the exam.

Topics Covered in the Exam

In this book, you will learn how to automate most common tasks you might find when administrating infrastructure using Ansible. Some of these tasks include:

- Understanding and use essential tools for handling files, directories, command-line environments, and documentation.
- Creating simple shell scripts.
- Operating running systems, including booting into different run levels, identifying processes, starting and stopping virtual machines, and controlling services.
- Configuring local storage using partitions and logical volumes.
- Creating and configuring filesystems and filesystem attributes, such as permissions, encryption, access control lists, and network filesystems.
- Deploying, configuring, and maintaining systems, including software installation, update, and core services.
- Managing users and groups.
- Managing security, including basic firewall and SELinux configuration.
- Performing basic container management.
- Configuring remote access using the web console and SSH.

- Configuring network interfaces and settings.
- Managing software using DNF.

While knowing these topics is important for exam certification, we are also introducing many of these concepts to make this book applicable for a wider audience.

Information About Certifications

For more information about the certification, suggested material, and additional resources related to Ansible, see Red Hat's official documentation (*https://oreil.ly/oJRrd*). The other certifications that you might take a look at are as follows:

Red Hat Certified System Administrator (https://oreil.ly/2iOk_)
: Red Hat Certified System Administrator (RHCSA) certifies that you can perform the core system administration.

Red Hat System Administration I (RH124) (https://oreil.ly/q5U8o)
: Red Hat System Administration I (RH124) is tailored for professionals with no prior experience in Linux system administration. It provides essential Linux administration skills by emphasizing fundamental tasks. Additionally, this course serves as a foundation for those aspiring to become full-time Linux system administrators, introducing critical command-line concepts and enterprise-grade tools.

Red Hat System Administration II (RH134) (https://oreil.ly/7QWyu)
: Red Hat System Administration II (RH134) builds on foundational Linux administration skills, focusing on advanced topics such as storage configuration and management, security management with SELinux, automation of recurring tasks, boot process management and troubleshooting, basic system performance tuning, and enhancing productivity through command-line automation.

Red Hat Certified System Administrator Rapid Track Course (https://oreil.ly/PcRcs)
: This course integrates the comprehensive content of Red Hat System Administration I (RH124) and Red Hat System Administration II (RH134), presenting the material in an accelerated format for an efficient review of key tasks.

Red Hat Enterprise Linux Automation with Ansible (RH294) (https://oreil.ly/K0JmF)
: Red Hat Enterprise Linux Automation with Ansible (RH294) is crafted for Linux administrators and developers aiming to streamline and automate repetitive, error-prone tasks such as system provisioning, configuration, application deployment, and orchestration.

Exam Details

This certification exam is not a typical test exam with a question and possible answers to choose from, but a hands-on, practical exam to perform real-world tasks using Ansible. You will need to create Ansible Playbooks and use them to configure systems for specific roles and behaviors in an environment provided for you. The playbook will be executed, and finally, a process will verify that those systems and services work as specified in the exam.

Please take your seat, and let's dive in.

CHAPTER 2

Introduction to Ansible

Ansible is an automation tool for managing your infrastructure elements such as cloud, virtual or bare metal servers, network, and application configuration. Like other automation tools, Ansible uses a code-first approach to describe the state of your infrastructure, so you can expect the same result every time you run it.

Ansible focuses on three important topics to make it the perfect tool for your IT operations:

- Ansible provides instructions to *automate* operations.
- Ansible provides *configuration management*.
- Ansible lets you automate the *deployment* of your applications into the infrastructure.

This chapter is one of the most important in the book because you'll get the ground knowledge to understand the rest of the book. You'll learn how Ansible works, the basic concepts on which Ansible is built, its architecture, and why it is essential to use. You'll also prepare your environment to run Ansible, and boot up some minimal virtual machines, which you'll use to run examples. Finally, you'll start executing your first Ansible commands to practice what you've learned in the chapter.

Ansible Overview

Before we discuss the more advanced capabilities of Ansible, it is important to understand what Ansible is, why it is used, and how it works. These concepts will be expanded upon in subsequent chapters.

Why Ansible?

In the past, you may have managed only a small number of servers, for example, two web servers, two database servers, and one proxy instance. Nowadays, things are more complex, with options such as cloud, virtual, and bare metal infrastructures. Applications are bigger and distributed, meaning that requirements for infrastructure are higher than ever before. This implies that there are now more servers to install, configure, and manage.

Due to the increased complexity of infrastructure, managing these resources manually is simply not an option anymore. Changes applied manually can introduce errors with unintended consequences, invalidating the state of the entire environment. Automation is the key to maintaining this complexity under control. Moreover, Ansible lets you store your infrastructure as code, making it maintainable and reproducible every time. So, how does Ansible work to communicate with nodes and execute operations against them?

Ansible Nodes

Ansible, unlike other solutions, uses a push-out approach, meaning that instructions are transmitted from a central location to each of the managed instances (or hosts). One of the big advantages of this approach is that the remote (or managed) machines need no specialized software (or agent) to be installed; Ansible is considered to be an *agentless* technology. Also, this approach keeps nodes more performant, as no extra software is installed, and more secure because you are eliminating a vector attack from the node. Ansible also supports a pull approach, but this is not the default, so we won't cover it.

When you want to start using Ansible, you first set up a *control node*. This is usually a local machine where you will install Ansible and store all the instructions to push out to the *managed nodes*.

The control node connects to each of the different managed nodes and applies all the instructions defined for each case, for example, installing system packages, copying some files from the control to the managed node, adding users, and so on. This communication occurs over the network, usually (but not always) over the SSH protocol, making all these interactions secure.

Linux/Unix hosts use SSH by default, while Windows hosts are configured with WinRM or OpenSSH.

Figure 2-1 shows the communication between a control node and the managed nodes.

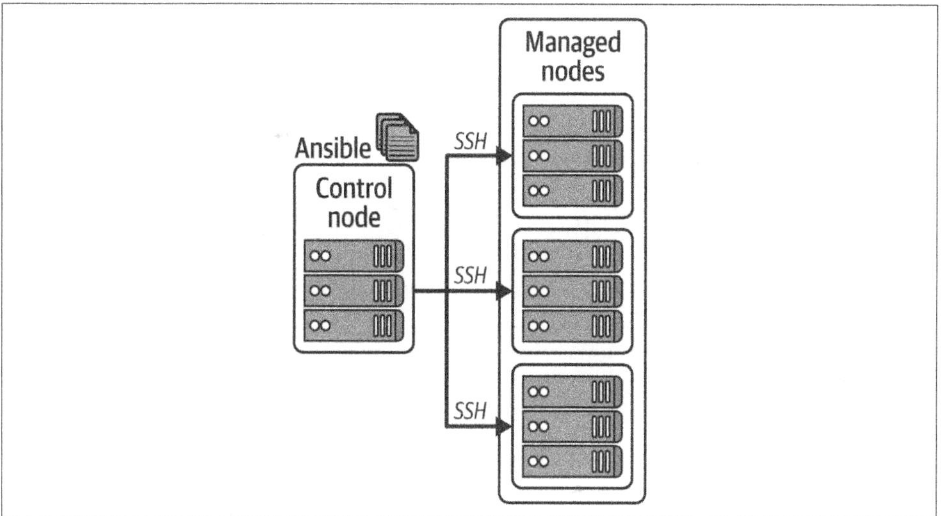

Figure 2-1. Control nodes and managed nodes

We've been talking about instructions and executing instructions against the managed nodes, but what are these instructions?

Ansible Modules

Ansible connects to managed nodes and pushes out small programs called *modules*, which implement the logic to execute against the node. Examples include running the `yum` command to install a package, or running `scp` or `sftp` to copy a file from the control node to the managed node. Figure 2-2 depicts the scenario where Ansible copies the modules to the managed nodes.

Once Ansible is connected to the nodes, it transfers the modules required by your instructions to the remote node(s) for execution. Then, these modules are executed, and Ansible removes them when it finishes.

Ansible comes with a set of built-in modules that provide support for most of the common tasks that you will need. However, you can also source modules from external sources or create custom modules of your own to extend the capabilities provided by Ansible. Modules are typically written using Python or PowerShell when targeting Windows instances.

With these concepts in mind, let's prepare your local machine to be suitable for running Ansible.

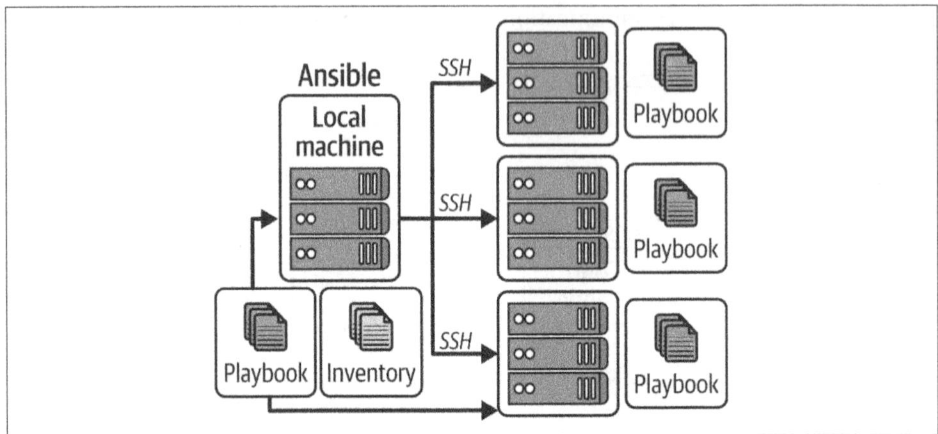

Figure 2-2. Control node copies modules to managed nodes

Installing and Running Ansible

This section will walk you through the steps for running Ansible on your local machine (control node) and configuring a virtual machine to run it as a managed node. In terms of hardware, for running Ansible standalone, you only need 1 CPU, 2 GB of memory, and 20 GB of hard disk space. But for this book, you'll need additional hardware resources in order to run a virtual machine as a managed node. So, the recommended settings for this environment are 2–4 CPUs, 8–16 GB of memory, and 40 GB of hard disk space.

Ansible has a different set of requirements for control nodes and managed nodes. Control nodes can be installed on any Unix machine with Python 3.9 or later installed, as well as on Windows machines using Windows Subsystem for Linux (WSL) installed. Windows environments without WSL are not currently (as of this writing) supported.

Managed nodes, however, do allow for additional flexibility in terms of the software requirements that can be used. Python 2 (2.7) or 3 (3.5–3.11) are both supported. The examples in this book have been tested and run on macOS Ventura 13.5.1 and Python 3.9.6. The following snippet shows how to verify the installed version of Python:

```
python3 -V

Python 3.9.6 (default, May  7 2023, 23:32:44)
```

Installing Ansible

As we previously mentioned, Ansible is an agentless automation tool. Once Ansible is installed, it does not add any third-party tooling, such as a database. Ansible is just another CLI tool that is installed on your machine (control node).

There are three options for installing Ansible on a control node:

- Install the release with your OS package manager (`yum`, `dnf`, `apt`, `pkg`, etc.).
- Install with `pip` (the Python package manager).
- Install from source or tarballs.

For example, in Fedora or RHEL, you'll use `dnf` to install Ansible, as shown in the following snippet:

```
sudo dnf install ansible
```

In Ubuntu/Debian-based systems, you might use `apt`, as shown in the following snippet:

```
sudo apt update
sudo apt install software-properties-common
sudo apt-add-repository --yes --update ppa:ansible/ansible
sudo apt install ansible
```

The preferred way to install Ansible on a macOS is with `pip`:

```
pip install --user ansible
```

Your machine must have `pip/pip3` installed (*https://oreil.ly/lPaal*).

In this Ansible document (*https://oreil.ly/pqCBU*), you can review the installation process for each of the supported systems. When writing this book, we used the Ansible 2.15.2 version, but any other supported version should work:

```
ansible --version

ansible [core 2.15.2]
```

Remote Machine Setup

Although Ansible only needs to be installed into the control node (usually your local machine), the remote machines have two minimal requirements:

- Access to the host using SSH (SSHD)
- Python 2 (version 2.7 or later) or Python 3 (version 3.5 or later)

Ansible manages remote machines using SSH. For running Ansible examples, you'll need a remote machine to connect and apply the instructions defined in the Ansible files (i.e., install a package, copy some files, create users, and so on)

In the real world, this remote machine might be a virtual machine, a cloud virtual machine, or a physical machine in a data center. Since you need a remote machine to use Ansible, in this section, you'll start two virtual machines from your local machine to make it a more generic example, and run from your development machine without requiring any external components.

Host and guest machines

When using virtual machines, you need to be aware of two important concepts, the guest and the host machine:

Host
: The physical machine where you install the operating system that manages the computer. In the scope of this book, it's your machine.

Guest
: The virtual machine that is installed, executed, and hosted on the host physical machine.

Figure 2-3 shows a schema of host/guest machine interaction.

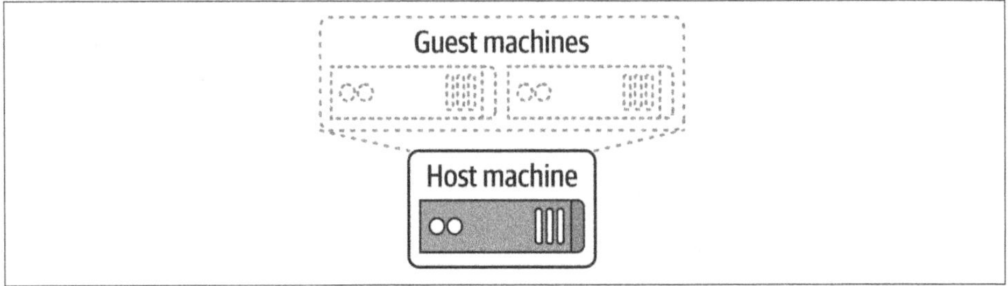

Figure 2-3. Host and guest machines

Even though you can use any other hypervisor to run a virtual machine, we decided to use the Oracle VM VirtualBox (*https://virtualbox.org*) as it's widely adopted and supported on most platforms.

Oracle VM VirtualBox

Oracle VM VirtualBox is a type-2 hypervisor for x86 virtualization that runs virtual machines on the local computer, and depending on the machine, enables virtualization in the BIOS. VirtualBox can load multiple guest operating systems under a single host operating system (host OS). Each guest can be started, paused, and stopped independently within its virtual machine.

To install VirtualBox, go to the VirtualBox download page (*https://oreil.ly/2CMq6*), select your operating system version, and install it. Figure 2-4 shows the VirtualBox home page with download options. Once installed, you don't need to do anything else, as Vagrant (*https://vagrantup.com*) will be used to create, start, and manage the virtual machines.

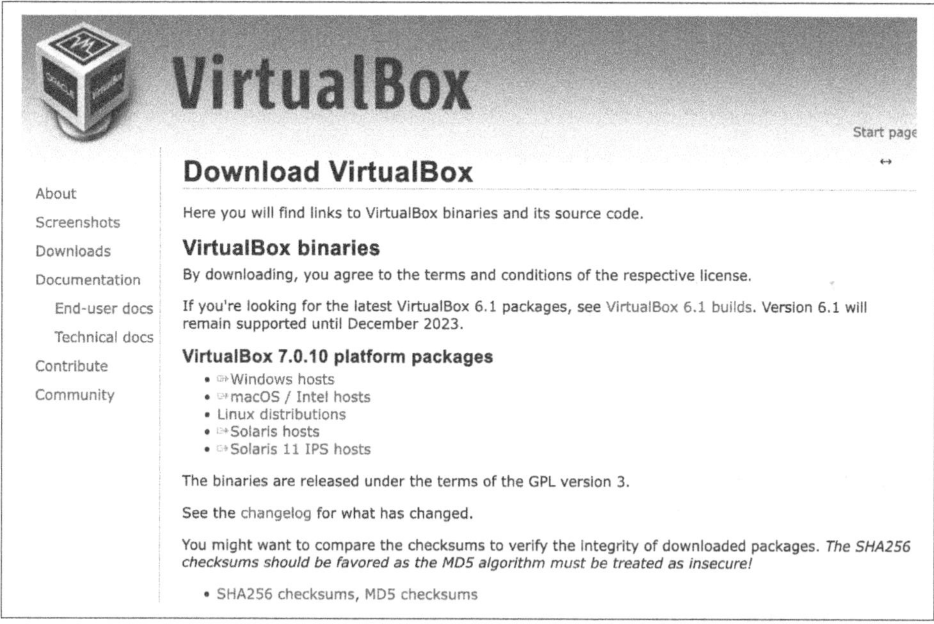

Figure 2-4. VirtualBox home page

Vagrant

Vagrant is an open source software solution for building and maintaining portable virtual software development environments. To install Vagrant, go to the Vagrant download page (*https://oreil.ly/LqRhO*), select your operative system package, and install it. Figure 2-5 depicts the Vagrant home page with download options.

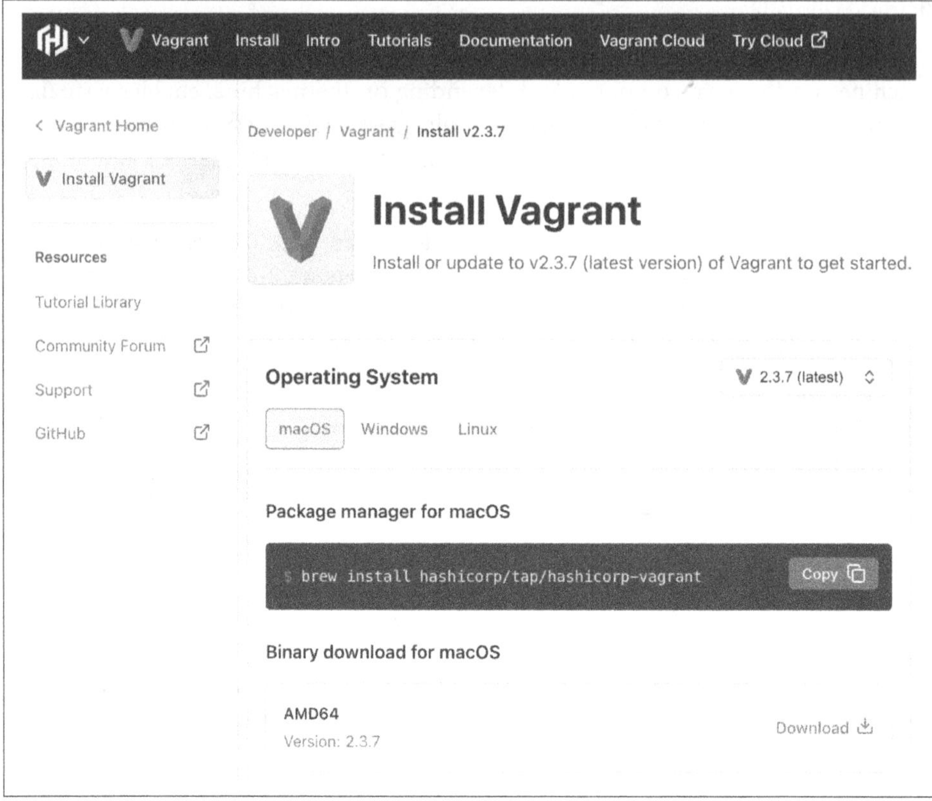

Figure 2-5. Vagrant home page

Once the installation process finishes, open a new terminal and run the following command to validate that Vagrant has been installed successfully:

```
vagrant --version
```

```
Vagrant 2.3.4
```

Next, before you can start the virtual machines, you need to create a *Vagrantfile* to define and configure the virtual machines and their supporting resources, including networking.

Let's create a new file named *Vagrantfile* configuring two virtual machines called `staging` and `prod`, based on the Fedora operating system, and creating a public network between the guest machines and the host machine:

```
# -*- mode: ruby -*-
# vi: set ft=ruby :
Vagrant.configure("2") do |config|
```

```
  config.vm.define "staging" do |staging| ❶

    staging.vm.box = "fedora/37-cloud-base" ❷
    staging.vm.box_version = "37.20221105.0"

    staging.ssh.password="vagrant" ❸

    staging.vm.network "public_network", use_dhcp_assigned_default_route: true ❹
    staging.ssh.forward_agent = true

    staging.vm.provision "shell", inline: "ip -4 -o a" ❺
  end

  config.vm.define "prod" do |prod| ❻
    prod.vm.box = "fedora/37-cloud-base"
    prod.vm.box_version = "37.20221105.0"
    prod.ssh.password="vagrant"
    prod.vm.network "public_network", use_dhcp_assigned_default_route: true
    prod.ssh.forward_agent = true
    prod.vm.provision "shell", inline: "ip -4 -o a"
  end


  config.vm.provider "virtualbox" do |vb|
    vb.memory = "2048" ❼
  end
end
```

❶ Defines the `staging` machine

❷ Sets Fedora from the Vagrant hosted box marketplace as the operating system

❸ Sets the password for the SSH connection (username is `vagrant` by default)

❹ Configures a public network between the guest and host (same IP space)

❺ Executes a shell script to print the IP address in the guest machine

❻ Defines the `prod` machine

❼ Sets the memory value for each machine

To start both machines, run the following command within the same directory as the *Vagrantfile*:

```
vagrant up
```

If you have more than one network adapter in your machine (i.e., LAN and WiFi), it's important to note that you'll need to choose the network adapter to which the machine should be assigned.

Select the adapter with the active internet connection so that the gateway is automatically configured to access the internet when downloading content is required. The output should be similar to the following:

```
Bringing machine 'staging' up with 'virtualbox' provider...
Bringing machine 'prod' up with 'virtualbox' provider...
==> staging: Importing base box 'fedora/37-cloud-base'...
==> staging: Matching MAC address for NAT networking...
==> staging: Checking if box 'fedora/37-cloud-base' version '37.20221105.0' is
up to date...
==> staging: Setting the name of the VM: vagrant_staging_1677076653292_56104
==> staging: Clearing any previously set network interfaces...
==> staging: Available bridged network interfaces: ❶
1) en0: Wi-Fi (AirPort)
2) en2: Thunderbolt 2
3) en1: Thunderbolt 1
4) bridge0
5) p2p0
6) awdl0
7) llw0
==> staging: When choosing an interface, it is usually the one that is
==> staging: being used to connect to the internet.
==> staging:
    staging: Which interface should the network bridge to? 1
==> staging: Preparing network interfaces based on configuration...
    staging: Adapter 1: nat
    staging: Adapter 2: bridged
==> staging: Forwarding ports...
    staging: 22 (guest) => 2222 (host) (adapter 1)
==> staging: Running 'pre-boot' VM customizations...
==> staging: Booting VM...
==> staging: Waiting for machine to boot. This may take a few minutes...
    staging: SSH address: 127.0.0.1:2222
    staging: SSH username: vagrant
...
    staging: 1: lo    inet 127.0.0.1/8 scope host lo\       valid_lft forever
    preferred_lft forever
    staging: 2: eth0    inet 10.0.2.15/24 brd 10.0.2.255 scope global dynamic
    noprefixroute eth0\       valid_lft 86398sec preferred_lft 86398sec
    staging: 3: eth1    inet 192.168.1.92/24 brd 192.168.1.255 scope global
    dynamic noprefixroute eth1\       valid_lft 43198sec preferred_lft 43198sec
==> prod: Importing base box 'fedora/37-cloud-base'...
==> prod: Matching MAC address for NAT networking...
==> prod: Checking if box 'fedora/37-cloud-base' version '37.20221105.0' is up
to date...
==> prod: Setting the name of the VM: vagrant_prod_1677076756188_18776
==> prod: Fixed port collision for 22 => 2222. Now on port 2200.
...
```

```
==> prod: Rsyncing folder: /Users/asotobu/git/ansible-tutorial/apps/vagrant/
=> /vagrant
==> prod: Running provisioner: shell...
    prod: Running: inline script
    prod: 1: lo    inet 127.0.0.1/8 scope host lo\       valid_lft forever
    preferred_lft forever
    prod: 2: eth0    inet 10.0.2.15/24 brd 10.0.2.255 scope global dynamic
    noprefixroute eth0\       valid_lft 86397sec preferred_lft 86397sec
    prod: 3: eth1    inet 192.168.1.93/24 brd 192.168.1.255 scope global
    dynamic noprefixroute eth1\       valid_lft 43198sec preferred_lft
    43198sec ❷
```

❶ Requests for the network interface

❷ Prints the list of assigned IPs for the machine

Use the `vagrant` tool to open an SSH connection to each machine, and execute the `ifconfig` tool to get the network information from each machine. For example, to get the IP of the `prod` virtual machine, you should execute the following command:

```
vagrant ssh prod -c "ifconfig"

eth0: flags=4163<UP,BROADCAST,RUNNING,MULTICAST>  mtu 1500
        inet 10.0.2.15  netmask 255.255.255.0  broadcast 10.0.2.255
        inet6 fe80::e248:38f1:e906:ab80  prefixlen 64  scopeid 0x20<link>
        ether 52:54:00:86:4c:24  txqueuelen 1000  (Ethernet)
        RX packets 1127  bytes 129961 (126.9 KiB)
        RX errors 0  dropped 0  overruns 0  frame 0
        TX packets 922  bytes 145449 (142.0 KiB)
        TX errors 0  dropped 0 overruns 0  carrier 0  collisions 0
```

Before using Ansible against these machines, the final task is to test communicating with both virtual machines to confirm they are capable of establishing an SSH connection. Let's connect using the previous IPs, with username `vagrant` and password `vagrant`, to validate that we can log in to both virtual machines. Change the IP with your virtual machine IP:

```
ssh vagrant@192.168.1.92

The authenticity of host 192.168.1.92 (192.168.1.92)' can't be established.
ED25519 key fingerprint is SHA256:CW3D3uc0+i77Fmcwk5Iskdrr98d70ZCrq2HUBLLwmvM.
This key is not known by any other names
Are you sure you want to continue connecting (yes/no/[fingerprint])? yes
Warning: Permanently added '192.168.1.92' (ED25519) to the list of known hosts.
[vagrant@localhost ~]$
```

And `exit` from the guest terminal:

```
logout
Connection to 192.168.1.92 closed.
```

Repeat these steps with the `staging` virtual machine.

We'll use the IPs given by our host machine, which most likely differ from your assigned addresses. Substitute the IP addresses accordingly.

Cleaning Up

You can stop the virtual machines using the following command:

```
vagrant halt

==> prod: Attempting graceful shutdown of VM...
==> staging: Attempting graceful shutdown of VM...
```

If you plan to not use them anymore, run the `destroy` command to remove them from the local disk:

```
vagrant halt

==> prod: Attempting graceful shutdown of VM...
==> staging: Attempting graceful shutdown of VM...
❯ vagrant destroy
    prod: Are you sure you want to destroy the 'prod' VM? [y/N] y
==> prod: Destroying VM and associated drives...
    staging: Are you sure you want to destroy the 'staging' VM? [y/N] y
==> staging: Destroying VM and associated drives...
```

Now that you've built the infrastructure to run Ansible, let's explore the key concepts of Ansible and execute a few commands against the machines you've created in this section.

Core Ansible Components

Once installed, you can start using Ansible from your laptop. However, it is important to understand the four core components of Ansible: inventories, CLIs, hosts, and configuration options.

Although we will cover them in detail in other chapters, we will provide a brief introduction here so that you will be able to understand the first set of Ansible examples.

Hosts

As mentioned before, there are two kinds of hosts in Ansible: the *control* hosts and *managed* hosts. The control host is where the Ansible CLI is executed, and this can be your local machine, a CI/CD server machine, a container, or any host that can execute Ansible.

On the other hand, managed hosts, also referred to as *nodes*, are the target devices (servers, network appliances, or any computer) you want to configure with Ansible. In the previous section, when we introduced the Ansible CLI tool, you executed a module against a single machine or host. Still, Ansible lets you specify a group or groups of hosts.

The Ansible *inventory file* defines all the managed hosts and groups of managed hosts to run automation tasks. Because nodes are associated to one or more groups within inventories, you run commands (and playbooks) against specific hosts and/or groups. This makes applying a change to multiple hosts easier than applying the change host by host. For example, if you have three nodes (classified under the *backend* group), you can install a particular piece of software, such as Java, with a single command instead of repeating it individually against each host.

The inventory files are written in either *INI* or *YAML* format, but the most common format is INI. Hosts are defined by their DNS name, hostname, or IP.

Let's see an initial example of a simple inventory file defining both of the hosts you created earlier using Vagrant:

```
192.168.1.92
192.168.1.93
```

In this example, no group has been defined; all hosts are ungrouped. Even though no group is defined explicitly, Ansible implicitly creates two groups: `all` and `ungrouped`. The `all` group contains every host defined in the inventory file, grouped or not. The `ungrouped` group contains all hosts that do not have another group besides `all`; in the previous example, both hosts fall in this category.

The same example in the YAML file is shown in the following snippet:

```
ungrouped:
  hosts:
    192.168.1.92:
    192.168.1.93:
```

The default location for Ansible inventory is */etc/ansible/hosts*. If you set hosts there, you are setting the inventory globally, and it's unnecessary to specify the inventory file location using the `-i` option. You can override the default Ansible inventory file location by setting the new location in the `ANSIBLE_INVENTORY` environment variable or within an *ansible.cfg* file, which will be covered in detail later on.

Groups

Assume that the `192.168.1.92` host is a web server and the `192.168.1.93` host is a database server. You will probably need to apply different commands in each instance, so let's group them so they are identified in the inventory file.

To create a group, set a new INI section with the group's name in the file. An INI section is defined on a line in square brackets (`[` and `]`), with the section's name between the brackets.

Let's create an inventory file with two groups (`webservers` and `dbservers`):

```
[webservers]
192.168.1.92

[dbservers]
192.168.1.93
```

The equivalent inventory in YAML format is shown in the following snippet:

```
webservers:
  hosts:
    192.168.1.92:
dbservers:
  hosts:
    192.168.1.93:
```

You can set more than one host in each group, as shown in the following example:

```
[webservers]
web1.example.com
web2.example.com

[dbservers]
192.168.0.45
db2.example.com
db3.example.com
```

You can put the same host in more than one group; for example, one host can belong to both testing and performance groups.

Group names should follow the variable name format. In summary, a variable name can only include letters, numbers, and underscores. Python keywords or playbook keywords are not valid variable names. A variable name cannot begin with a number.

Table 2-1 shows valid and invalid variable names.

Table 2-1. Valid and invalid variable names

Valid	Invalid
foo	*foo
foo_env	async, environment (Python keyword)
foo_port	foo-port, foo.port, foo port
foo5, _foo	5foo, 46

Adding variables to inventory

Just as a programming language does, Ansible provides the concept of variables. A variable lets you change the behavior of a common function by providing a different value as an input parameter. For example, the admin password for a database server might be different in staging than in a production environment. But installing the database server itself should, for the most part, be the same. The password could be a variable that, depending on the environment, could have one value or another.

You can use variables in a variety of places, including *module arguments*, within *conditional* `when` statements, in *templates*, and in *loops*. Variables are set in multiple places in Ansible, one of which includes the inventory. In the inventory file, you can store variable values to apply to a specific host or group.

In Ansible, there are two kinds of variables:

User variables
: Variables you create, set, and use as part of your logic.

Special variables
: Variables provided by Ansible. You can use them to get information from Ansible (`inventory_file`, `groups`, and so on) as *magic variables*, or to set the connection details to hosts (`ansible_user`, `ansible_become_user`, `ansible_ssh_private_key_file`, and so on).

Let's set the Ansible user in the inventory file:

```
[webservers]
web1.example.com ansible_user=vagrant
```

Based on the previous inventory definition, Ansible uses the `vagrant` username instead of the system-provided value to establish the SSH connection against the managed host.

The equivalent in YAML format is as follows:

```
webservers:
  hosts:
    web1.example.com:
      ansible_user: vagrant
```

If all hosts in a group share a variable value, you can apply that variable to all groups at once. To define a variable to multiple hosts, you can place them in a special section that follows the format `<group_name>:vars`. For example, to change the Ansible port (this is the port Ansible uses for establishing the SSH connection) to a different value for all hosts defined in a group, define a new section with the `:vars` suffix, as shown in the following snippet:

```
[webservers]
web1.example.com
web2.example.com

[webservers:vars]
ansible_port=5555
```

The equivalent inventory in YAML format is as follows:

```
webservers:
  hosts:
    web1.example.com:
  vars:
    ansible_port: 5555
```

Multiple inventory files

As your inventory grows with more entries, you may need more than one file to organize your hosts and groups. There are four possible options you can choose beyond using a single file:

- You can create a directory with multiple inventory files.
- You can pull inventory dynamically, for example, hosts created in the cloud.
- You can use a mix of dynamic and static inventory files.
- You can use the `-i` argument multiple times to append inventory files.

We've covered the basics of creating and using inventories. We'll cover more advanced use cases in later chapters.

In the following section, you'll use the CLI tools provided by Ansible.

CLI Tools

When Ansible was installed (see "Installing Ansible" on page 9), the Ansible CLI tool and a few other CLI tools supporting the Ansible ecosystem were also installed. In this section, we'll provide an overview of two of the most important tools you'll use: `ansible` and `ansible-playbook`. We'll then briefly discuss a few other tools.

ansible CLI

The `ansible` tool defines and runs a single task against a set of hosts. This tool can be used in any situation. Still, because of its simplicity, it is mainly used for test/demo purposes or executing sporadic tasks (such as shutting down hosts).

Let's see an initial example of using the `ansible` tool. You'll use Ansible to ping the hosts you created earlier to validate that they are up and running.

First of all, create an inventory file called *inventory* with both host IPs defined:

```
192.168.1.92
192.168.1.93
```

Next, ping the hosts using the `ansible` tool with the previously defined inventory.

The `ansible` command format uses <pattern> as the first argument and then a list of optional arguments. The `-m` argument is used to specify an Ansible module (such as the ping module) to execute the logic of executing a ping to the host. If no module is set, it defaults to the command module, which executes a command against the selected hosts matched by the specified pattern.

The command(s) will *not* be processed through the shell.

In a terminal window, run the following command:

```
ansible all -i inventory -m ping

192.168.1.101 | UNREACHABLE! => {
    "changed": false,
    "msg": "Failed to connect to the host via ssh: asotobu@192.168.1.101:
    Permission denied (publickey,gssapi-keyex,gssapi-with-mic,password).",
    "unreachable": true

192.168.1.102 | UNREACHABLE! => {
    "changed": false,
    "msg": "Failed to connect to the host via ssh: asotobu@192.168.1.102:
    Permission denied (publickey,gssapi-keyex,gssapi-with-mic,password).",
    "unreachable": true
```

The command is failing because it is trying to connect using the current user logged in to the terminal, which, in our case, is `asotobu`. To fix it, you must specify the username to establish the SSH connection. Use the `--user` option of the `ansible` CLI with `vagrant` to override the default username.

Repeat the execution, but set the username:

```
ansible all -i inventory --user vagrant -m ping

192.168.1.101 | SUCCESS => {
    "ansible_facts": {
        "discovered_interpreter_python": "/usr/bin/python3"
    },
    "changed": false,
    "ping": "pong"

192.168.1.102 | SUCCESS => {
    "ansible_facts": {
        "discovered_interpreter_python": "/usr/bin/python3"
    },
    "changed": false,
    "ping": "pong"
```

If the unreachable error persists, add the --ask-pass argument in the command after the username.

Now, everything worked as expected; you executed a simple command that verified all managed hosts were up and running.

The ansible tool has an extensive list of optional arguments. Table 2-2 summarizes the most important ones.

Table 2-2. ansible optional arguments

Flag	Description
-i, --inventory	Specify inventory host path or a comma-separated host list.
-b, --become	Run operations with become (does not imply password prompting). When using this option, the user executing the Ansible command "becomes" another user, different from the user who logged in to the machine. It uses existing privilege escalation tools like sudo, su, pfexec, doas, pbrun, dzdo, ksu, runas, machinectl, and others.
-f <FORKS>, --forks <FORKS>	Specify the number of parallel processes to use. Defaults to 5.
-B <SECONDS>, --background <SECONDS>	Run asynchronously, failing after <SECONDS>.
-K, --ask-become-pass	Ask for a privilege escalation password.
--become-method <BECOME_METHOD>	Privilege escalation method to use. Defaults to sudo.

Flag	Description
`--become-password-file <BECOME_PASSWORD_FILE>`, `--become-pass-file <BECOME_PASSWORD_FILE>`	Privilege escalation password file.
`--become-user <BECOME_USER>`	Run operations as this user. Defaults to root.
`-e`, `--extra-vars`	Set additional variables as key=value or YAML/JSON. When specifying a file containing a set of variables, prepend the file with `@`.
`-m <MODULE_NAME>`, `--module-name <MODULE_NAME>`	Name of the module to execute. Defaults to `command`.
`-a <MODULE_ARGS>`, `--args <MODULE_ARGS>`	The module options in key=value format or JSON.
`--ask-vault-password`, `--ask-vault-pass`	Ask for the vault password.
`-v`, `-vv`, `-vvv`	Print more debug messages.

ansible-playbook

As described previously, the `ansible` tool is only used in certain circumstances (ad hoc commands); what you will use in most circumstances is the `ansible-playbook` tool. It is similar to the `ansible` tool but executes sets of tasks defined in Ansible playbooks against the targeted hosts instead of a single ad hoc command.

A playbook is a list of tasks executed automatically with limited manual effort across all the targeted hosts. In summary, playbooks tell Ansible what to do on which devices; for example, installing Java 17 hosts where the backend is deployed. We'll cover playbooks in detail in Chapter 3.

The format of the `ansible-playbook` command is a list of optional arguments and then at least the location of one playbook (but it can be a list). The `ansible-playbook` tool has an extensive list of optional arguments. Table 2-3 summarizes the most important ones.

Table 2-3. `ansible-playbook` optional arguments

Flag	Description
`-i`, `--inventory`	Specify inventory host path or comma-separated host list.
`-b`, `--become`	Run operations with `become` (does not imply password prompting). When using this option, the user executing the Ansible command "becomes" another user, different from the user who logged in to the machine. It uses existing privilege escalation tools like `sudo`, `su`, `pfexec`, `doas`, `pbrun`, `dzdo`, `ksu`, `runas`, `machinectl`, and others.
`-K`, `--ask-become-pass`	Ask for privilege escalation password.

Flag	Description
`--become-method <BECOME_METHOD>`	Privilege escalation method to use. Defaults to `sudo`.
`--become-password-file <BECOME_PASSWORD_FILE>`, `--become-pass-file <BECOME_PASSWORD_FILE>`	Privilege escalation password file.
`--become-user <BECOME_USER>`	Run operations as this user defaults to root.
`-f <FORKS>`, `--forks <FORKS>`	Specify the number of parallel processes to use. Defaults to 5.
`-e`, `--extra-vars`	Set additional variables as key=value or YAML/JSON. When specifying a file containing a set of variables, prepend the file with @.
`-t <TAGS>`, `--tags <TAGS>`	Only run plays and tasks tagged with these values.
`--skip-tags <SKIP_TAGS>`	Only run plays and tasks whose tags do not match these values.
`-l <SUBSET>`, `--limit <SUBSET>`	Further limit selected hosts to an additional pattern.
`-c <CONNECTION>`, `--connection <CONNECTION>`	Connection type to use. Defaults to smart.
`-u <REMOTE_USER>`, `--user <REMOTE_USER>`	Connect as the provided user. Defaults to None.
`--ask-vault-password`, `--ask-vault-pass`	Ask for the vault password.

Other CLI tools

The installation process copies `ansible` and `ansible-playbook` tools to your machine, but those are not the only tools Ansible provides. Here is a complete list of Ansible tools that are available for use. This is an introduction to each command; you'll learn more about them in other chapters:

`ansible-config`
: A CLI tool to initialize, list, view, or dump the configuration files.

`ansible-doc`
: Displays information related to the modules installed in Ansible libraries. It shows a terse listing of plug-ins and their short descriptions, provides a printout of their documentation, and can create a short *snippet* as an example, which can be pasted into a playbook.

`ansible-galaxy`
: Command to create, download, build, or publish Ansible roles and collections.

`ansible-inventory`
: Displays Ansible inventory information; by default, it uses the inventory script JSON format.

`ansible-pull`
: Pulls a remote copy of Ansible playbooks on each managed node, each set to run via `cron` and update the playbook source via a source repository. This inverts the default push architecture of Ansible into a pull architecture, which has near-limitless scaling potential.

`ansible-vault`
: Utility for encrypting/decrypting Ansible data files. Typically, you'll encrypt/decrypt Ansible variables (for example, usernames/passwords, application configuration files with sensitive information, and third-party API keys). Still, since Ansible tasks or handlers are data objects, these also can be encrypted.

In the following section, you will learn how to select the target hosts where Ansible executes the commands.

Host Patterns

When executing Ansible by either using the `ansible` tool or defining a playbook, you must select which nodes or groups Ansible will run against.

In the previous section, you used a pattern to select `all` hosts from the inventory to execute the command against. But this was just an example, as an Ansible pattern can refer to a single host, an IP address, an inventory group, or a set of groups defined within inventory files.

This section will teach you about various host patterns, from simple to advanced types. Simple patterns are enough, in most cases, to select hosts. But it is important to have a correct understanding of patterns as it might make a difference in solving a complex problem efficiently.

Let's assume an inventory file contains the following:

```
[webservers]
web1.example.com
web2.example.com

[dbservers]
db1.example.com
db2.example.com
db3.example.com

[staging]
web1.example.com
db1.example.com
```

To target all hosts you've seen before, use the `all` pattern; Ansible runs commands against all hosts defined in the inventory.

To target a specific host, use the hostname directly; for example, you could use `db1.example.com`. Target multiple hosts, separating them using a comma (`,`) or a colon (`:`), for example, `web1.example.com,db1.example.com`.

You can refer to a group by its name, `webservers`, to execute Ansible commands against all hosts belonging to the group. Or, you can also target more than one group, separating them with a colon (`:`), for example, `webservers:dbservers`.

Group patterns also support two operators: the excluding operator (`!`) and the inclusion operator (`&`). For example, the targeted host for the pattern `webservers:!staging` is `web2.example.com`, as `web1.example.com` is in the exclusion group. If you use the following pattern, `webservers:&staging`, the target host is `web1.example.com`, as it's the only host in both groups.

The following order is used when processing operators:

1. `:` and `,`
2. `&`
3. `!`

You can use wildcard patterns to specify a group of hosts directly. For example, `*.example.com` will match every host of the `example.com` domain.

You can use regular expressions instead of wildcards if you need to by starting the pattern with a (`~`) character, for example, `~(web|db).*\.example\.com`.

You can add dynamic patterns referring to elements as variables you set at runtime. For example, with the following pattern, `webservers:!{{ excluded }}`, excluded groups are set as an Ansible variable named `excluded`.

You can also refer to hosts using an array-like expression. Some examples include the following:

```
dbservers[0]        # db1.example.com
dbservers[-1]       # db3.example.com
dbservers[0:2]      # == db1.example.com, db2.example.com
dbservers[1:]       # == db2.example.com, db3.example.com
dbservers[:3]       # == db1.example.com, db2.example.com, db3.example.com
```

Patterns depend on inventory. If a host or group is not listed in your inventory, you cannot use a pattern to target it.

Another important Ansible concept is the configuration files that let you configure Ansible globally.

Configuring Ansible

You can configure Ansible via a configuration file affecting the overall execution. For example, you can set the `become` password file globally so that you do not need to type it repeatedly when running Ansible.

The default configuration parameters should be sufficient for most users. However, there are some situations in which you might want to customize how Ansible operates. The Ansible configuration is a file defined in INI format, using a hash sign (#) for line comments, and a semicolon (;) for line and inline comments. You can see an example in the following snippet, where the inventory source is set:

```
# line comment
inventory = /etc/ansible/hosts  ; Sets inventory file location
```

The Ansible configuration file can be set in different places and loaded in the following order:

- Set the `ANSIBLE_CONFIG` environment variable pointing to the configuration file.
- The *ansible.cfg* file created in the same directory where Ansible is executed.
- The *~/.ansible.cfg* file located at the root of your home directory.
- The */etc/ansible/ansible.cfg* global file at the default Ansible directory.

An extensive list of properties can be set in an Ansible configuration file. They are all defined in the official documentation (*https://oreil.ly/IJto7*).

Since managing Ansible configuration properties might be complicated and you can be overwhelmed by the sheer number of options, Ansible provides the `ansible-config` CLI tool that enables you to scaffold an *ansible.cfg* file. It can also be used as a helping tool for checking possible configuration options, its default values, and a description of its usage.

To generate a complete configuration file example, run the following command in a terminal window:

```
ansible-config init --disabled > ansible.cfg
```

The generated file is a commented-out example describing the settings and valid values for each property. To enable any property, remove the comment.

To list all available options, run:

```
ansible-config list
```

The output is a scrolling page describing each of the settings.

To print all the current values used during Ansible execution, use the `dump` option:

```
ansible-config dump
```

The output is a scrolling page showing each key with the value used at runtime.

After executing your first Ansible command (an ad hoc command) and exploring the basics of Ansible, it's time to understand ad hoc commands in further detail.

Ad Hoc Commands

In the previous section, you executed the `ping` command to all hosts defined in the inventory file using the `ansible` CLI tool. This scenario is known in Ansible as an `ad hoc` command.

Ad hoc commands show how easy it is to apply a single task on one or more managed nodes. They are compelling and let you automate some operations, but they have some limitations:

- Only a single task can be executed.
- The steps are not reusable nor can they be versioned within a source control repository, as the CLI-based commands are imperatively executed on a control node.

In Chapter 3, we will discuss *playbooks*, which solve these challenges. However, even with these limitations, ad hoc commands are still very useful. Ad hoc commands take the following form:

```
ansible \ ❶
        <pattern> \ ❷
        <ansible arguments> \ ❸
        -m <module> \ ❹
        -a "<module arguments>" ❺
```

❶ `ansible` CLI tool

❷ Host pattern

❸ Arguments of the tool (`-i`, `-b`, etc.)

❹ Module to execute (i.e., `ping`)

❺ Module arguments; accept options either through the `key=value` syntax or a JSON.

Commands Versus Shell

If you do not specify the module option (`-m`), Ansible will rely on using the *command* module. The command module executes a command against the managed host. The argument of this module is the command to execute, along with its arguments. The command must be available within the managed host, and the SSH user has the rights to execute it.

The command module does not support extended shell syntax like piping (`|`), shell variables (`$HOSTNAME`), and redirects (>, <, &). If you need a shell environment, use the *shell* module instead, for example, `ansible staging -m ansible.builtin.shell -a 'echo $HOSTNAME'`.

Let's see some examples where the ad hoc command is useful.

Rebooting Servers

One such use case where ad hoc commands can help is the halting, stopping, or rebooting of servers. To reboot all managed servers defined in the inventory file, run the following command:

```
ansible all -i inventory -a "/sbin/reboot"
```

If the user doesn't have permissions to execute the rebooting command, privilege escalation is required to become another user with the necessary permissions to reboot the server, such as `root`. Here, Ansible executes the the command under the `root` user:

```
ansible all -i inventory -a "/sbin/reboot" -u root \
  --become --ask-become-pass
```

If you use `--ask-become-pass`, Ansible prompts you for the password for privilege escalation. The command reboots the given server, so the connection with Ansible is stopped.

Managing Users

The `user` command allows for the creation, management, and removal of user accounts on managed nodes.

Let's see how to add a new user to all machines using an ad hoc command:

```
ansible all -i inventory -u root --become --ask-become-pass -m user -a \
  "name=ada password=<crypted password here>"
```

Here is the equivalent command using JSON-formatted arguments:

```
ansible all -i ungrouped_inventory --user vagrant  -m user -a '{"name":"ada", \
  "password":<crypted password here>}'
```

Removing a user is just as easy:

```
ansible all -i inventory -m ansible.builtin.user -a "name=john state=absent"
```

Later on, you will learn about *states* in Ansible. For now, think of states as how to set the desired result of a resource once Ansible execution has completed. In the above example, since state was specified to be `absent`, the result after Ansible has completed executing is the removal of the user from the host.

Gathering Facts

In some situations, you might need details associated with hosts in your inventory. Ansible organizes these details into *facts*. Facts are remote host information, such as the hostname, IPs, disk, disk space, date time, bios, and so on. You can use these facts later in a playbook.

Let's gather facts from the two virtual machines you created at the beginning of this chapter, using the `setup` module:

```
ansible all -i inventory -m ansible.builtin.setup

192.168.1.102 | SUCCESS => {
    "ansible_facts": {
        "ansible_all_ipv4_addresses": [
            "10.0.2.15",
            "192.168.1.102"
        ],
        "ansible_all_ipv6_addresses": [
            "fe80::e248:38f1:e906:ab80",
            "fd9c:3006:46b1:318:16d5:ffce:8307:bc52",
            "fe80::17e:a1e:12c7:e295"
        ]

...
```

The output is in JSON format, providing all kinds of information about the host.

Conclusion

With a basic understanding of Ansible, basic concepts like inventory, and how to execute Ansible modules, it's time to move on and learn how to use Ansible to write tasks as code and automate their execution.

In the following chapter, we'll introduce one of the most important concepts of Ansible: *playbooks*.

CHAPTER 3

Ansible Playbooks

In Chapter 2, we provided an overview of when ad hoc commands are helpful. However, in most cases, you will need to perform more complex actions that involve running multiple tasks instead of just one. In addition, it is important to ensure that every time we invoke our automation, we can expect the same result.

To accomplish these goals, you will require an Ansible Playbook. Playbooks are the core of Ansible. In the chapter, you will learn what an Ansible Playbook is, and see the most common parts of a playbook that you might encounter or need. You will also run your first playbook.

Finally, you'll create a very simple web application, and you'll deploy to a virtual machine using Ansible.

What Is an Ansible Playbook?

An Ansible Playbook is a list of *tasks* that are automatically executed for a specified set of nodes. One or more Ansible tasks can be combined to make a *play*. A play consists of an ordered set of tasks to execute against host selections from the Ansible inventory file. A *playbook* can include one or more plays.

The most important part of a playbook is a task, which represents a call to an Ansible *module*. We've already seen modules in the previous chapter; for example, when you were pinging a host, you did so using the *ping* module. Or, when creating a new user within a host, you used the *user* module.

Finally, a playbook contains the managed hosts where Ansible executes the modules. Figure 3-1 contains an overview of each of the elements of an Ansible playbook.

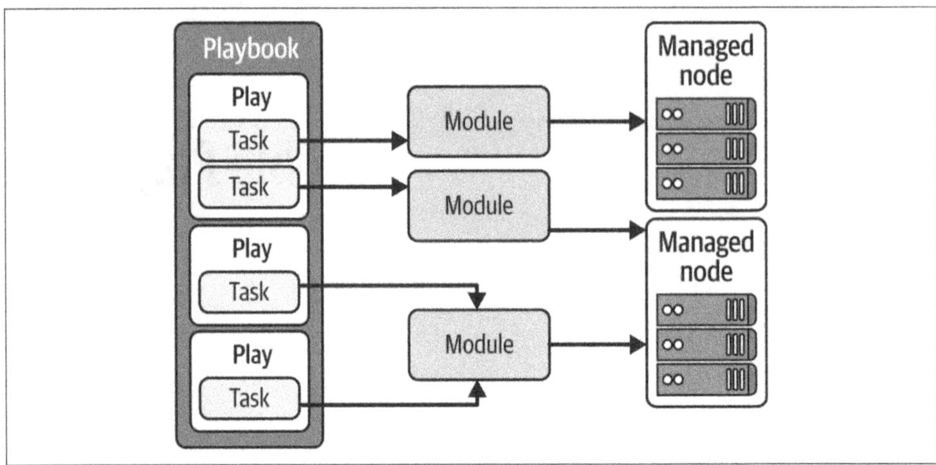

Figure 3-1. Playbook elements

There are plenty of different modules that you can use, such as:

yum
: To run the `yum` command to install a package on a Fedora/RHEL machine.

copy
: To copy a file from the control node to the managed node.

service
: To manage services (those managed by init systems).

command
: To execute a command against a target host.

Of course, there are plenty of other modules that we will touch upon throughout the course of this book.

An Example Playbook

A playbook is a YAML file containing one or more tasks executed against managed hosts. Apart from tasks and other elements, the core goal of a playbook is to define a system's desired *state*.

Most Ansible modules are *idempotent*, which means they check whether the desired final state has already been achieved. If it's achieved, the task is not executed, avoiding repeating the task execution.

So, when defining tasks, if the module supports idempotency through the *state* module option, it's always important to determine the current state to ensure that the desired state is met when the execution of the module is complete. Examples of desired states might be a running service, a created or deleted directory, or an installed package.

Let's create a simple playbook named *playbook.yaml* containing two plays:

- First play installs (or updates) to the latest Apache Server.
- Second play installs (or updates) to the latest PostgreSQL server and ensures it's started using the init system (systemd, upstart, OpenRC, etc.) installed in the Linux distribution.

The content is shown in the following snippet:

```
---
- name: Web Servers ❶
  hosts: webservers ❷
  become: true ❸

  tasks: ❹
  - name: Ensure apache is at the latest version
    ansible.builtin.yum: ❺
      name: httpd  ❻
      state: latest ❼

- name: DB servers
  hosts: databases
  become: true

  tasks:
  - name: Ensure postgresql is at the latest version
    ansible.builtin.yum:
      name: postgresql
      state: latest
  - name: Ensure that postgresql is started
    ansible.builtin.service: ❽
      name: postgresql
      state: started ❾
```

❶ Sets the name of the first play

❷ Defines the group of hosts to execute against

❸ Executes tasks with elevated privilege

❹ Defines the tasks to execute in the current play

❺ Declares the yum module will be used for the task

❻ Installs the `httpd` package

❼ Defines the most recent version of the package to install

❽ Declares the `service` module will be used for the task

❾ Ensures that PostgreSQL service is started

This is just an initial example. Keep in mind that we have yet to introduce all of the concepts of a playbook, but it should be fairly easy to understand what a playbook is doing.

For Windows, use the `ansible.windows.win_service` module instead when looking to manage Windows services.

Now, define an inventory with both host groups present:

```
[webservers]
web1.example.com
web2.example.com

[databases]
db1.example.com
db2.example.com
```

Executing a playbook

To execute the playbook with this inventory, use the `ansible-playbook` command:

```
ansible-playbook -i inventory playbook.yaml
```

This command, while simple, executes a number of complex operations under the hook as defined in the playbook.

If you want to run this command with the virtual machines created previously, you would need to update the inventory with the target hostnames.

By default, Ansible executes each task in the order it is defined within the playbook, one at a time, against all machines matched by the host pattern. The task is executed in parallel against all machines, and when finished, Ansible moves on to the next task until no more tasks are left. There are options (or strategies) that can be used to change this behavior, especially to debug a playbook.

Execution strategies

Ansible execution is versatile enough that you can modify how and when tasks are executed. By specifying parameters at the playbook level, play level, or task level, you gain control over how tasks are run within a playbook. Let's explore all of them by providing a few examples to demonstrate their use.

In Ansible, there are three execution strategies:

`linear`
: This is the default. The task is executed simultaneously against all hosts using five forks (by default), and then the next series of hosts until the batch is done before going on to the next task.

`debug`
: Task execution is like the linear strategy but controlled by an interactive debug session.

`free`
: Ansible will not wait for other hosts to finish the current task before queuing more tasks for other hosts. It prevents blocking new tasks for hosts that have already completed.

Strategies can be specified at the play level or globally.

At the play level, the `strategy` parameter can be set at the same level as the `hosts` or `tasks` parameters:

```
- name: Web Servers
  hosts: webservers
  strategy: free ❶

  tasks:
  #...

- name: DB servers
  hosts: databases
  #...
```

❶ Sets the `free` strategy for the `webservers` play

Globally, you can set the strategy within the *ansible.cfg* file under the `defaults` group:

```
[defaults] ❶
strategy = free ❷
```

❶ "Default" group configuration properties

❷ Sets the `free` strategy

Forks

Ansible uses the concept of *forks* to determine the maximum number of simultaneous connections made for each task. This can affect the number of parallel hosts a task is executed against.

By default, the number of forks is five, meaning that Ansible only establishes five SSH connections for each task simultaneously to five different hosts. If, for example, there is only one host, then Ansible will only do one SSH connection.

According to the Ansible documentation, a good fork value is 25 as it behaves well in most scenarios.

There are two methods to set forks globally: in the *Ansible.cfg* file or as a CLI parameter.

Within the *ansible.cfg* file, `forks` can be set as shown in the following example:

```
[defaults] ❶
forks = 50 ❷
```

❶ Default group configuration properties

❷ Sets to 50 forks

As a CLI command, forks can be specified using the `--forks` parameter:

```
ansible-playbook playbook.yaml --forks 50
```

Setting the Batch Size

You can also set the number of nodes processed in tasks within a single run. In forks, the value is set primarily due to hardware limitations. However, in the `serial` property, the number of parallel executions is typically based on a software/application restriction. For example, during a rolling update, you could define how many hosts Ansible should manage simultaneously to avoid downtime.

The serial value can be expressed as an absolute value (i.e., three nodes each time), as a percentage (i.e., 30% of the hosts), or by batch (i.e., 1, 5, 10 will execute the first batch with 1 host, the second with 5 hosts, and third with 10 hosts).

The `serial` property is set at the play level, which affects each of the defined tasks, executing all of them in the same batch before moving to the following host batch. For example, given the following playbook file:

```
---
- name: serial example play
  hosts: webservers
  serial: 4 ❶

  tasks: ❷
    - name: first task
      ansible.builtin.command: hostname
    - name: second task
      ansible.builtin.command: hostname
```

❶ Sets `serial` to 4 hosts

❷ Defines two tasks in this play

Assuming the `webservers` group has eight hosts, Ansible executes the play entirely (both first and second tasks) on the first four hosts, and when both tasks finish, moves on to the next group of four hosts.

Modifying the `serial` value changes the scope of the Ansible failures to the batch size, not the entire host list. To modify this behavior, you can use the `ignore_unreachable` or `max_fail_percentage` configuration properties.

As noted before, you can set a percentage instead of an absolute value. The following snippet shows how to configure a batch size of 50% of the hosts specified in the `webservers` group:

```
---
- name: serial example play
  hosts: webservers
  serial: "50%" ❶

  tasks:
  #...
```

❶ Defines the percentage of hosts affected

You can also specify batch sizes as a list of absolute and/or percentage values, and even mix absolute and percentage numbers.

In the following snippet, you can see a batch definition using absolute values. Ansible executes the first batch with the first host, the next contains three hosts, and (if there are any hosts left) every batch afterward contains either five hosts or all the remaining hosts:

```
---
- name: serial example play
```

```
hosts: webservers
serial: ❶
  - 1
  - 3
  - 5
```

❶ Defines `serial` as a list

Ordering Execution Based on Inventory

Previously, we introduced you to executing tasks in a batch of hosts. But when a `serial` value of 3 is specified and there is an inventory of 20 hosts, which hosts will be in the first batch of 3, the second one, and so on?

By default, there is no guarantee the execution order of tasks against hosts/groups is the same as defined in the inventory source file. In most simple cases it is, but in complex scenarios Ansible might use other approaches.

With the `order` keyword, you can modify the algorithm used to choose the hosts. The possible values are:

`inventory`
: This is the default mode, as explained above.

`reverse_inventory`
: This is the same as the default, but in the reverse order.

`sorted`
: Sorted alphabetically by name.

`reverse_sorted`
: As `sorted`, but in reverse order.

`shuffle`
: Randomly ordered on each run.

An example of configuring the `order` property is shown in the following snippet:

```
- hosts: all ❶
  order: sorted ❷
  tasks:
  # ...
```

❶ Special keyword to execute against all hosts defined in the inventory

❷ Sets the order to the `sorted` value

Running on a single machine

In some rare cases, you might run a task only with the first host in the batch of hosts. For example, in database schema updates, you only want to run on one host of the database cluster. To do this approach, Ansible provides the `run_once` property to execute the task against only one node:

```
tasks:
  - command: "flyway -url='' -user='' migrate"
    run_once: true ❶
```

❶ Setting to `true` executes the task once per host (in the batch of hosts).

To run a task on a specified host, instead of the first host in the batch, there is also the `delegate_to` property to set exactly the hostname where Ansible executes the task:

```
tasks:
  - ansible.builtin.command: "flyway -url='' -user='' migrate"
    run_once: true
    delegate_to: db1.example.com ❶
```

❶ This task executes against the `db1` host.

Tasks marked as `run_once` will be run on one host in each serial batch. For example, assuming `serial` is set to 5, and the inventory file contains 10 hosts, then there will be 2 batches of execution.

This means the command will be executed twice, once for every first host of the batch. If you want to avoid this behavior and execute the task only once regardless of the batch size, use the conditional `when` keyword.

We introduce conditionals and control flow in later chapters.

Restricting execution

Earlier in this chapter, you learned how to restrict the number of forks globally or per play. But, sometimes, due to the nature of the command being executed, you might need to limit the number of workers for a specific command. The `throttle` keyword limits the number of workers for a particular task.

An example of `throttle` is shown in the following snippet:

```
tasks:
  - ansible.builtin.command: /path/to/cpu_intensive_command
    throttle: 1
```

At this point, you have an introduction to Ansible playbooks, why they are important, and how they are executed. Next, you will learn the structure of a playbook, the primary sections, and how they should be used.

Structure of Ansible Playbooks

In the previous section, you were introduced to a playbook composed of plays, each containing tasks. But playbooks can contain other elements that will help make them easier to maintain. Even more important, you can enable them to be reused for different use cases. Now, let's look at the structure of a playbook in further detail.

An Example Playbook Structure

This is just an overview of each playbook part and its structure. Some of the contents are complex, and we'll explain in further detail as we go along.

The following example contains a playbook that:

- Defines two variables.
- Imports the MongoDB collection to run tasks against a MongoDB (local) instance.
- Registers and executes a role that installs Java 1.8.0.
- Defines a handler that restarts the httpd service.
- Creates five tasks, installing and managing multiple systems.

Let's see this in code:

```
---
- name: Web Servers
  hosts: webservers
  become: true
  remote_user: root ❶
  vars: ❷
    username: Ada
    password: Alexandra
  collections:
    - community.mongodb
  roles: ❸
    - role: geerlingguy.java
      java_packages:
        - java-1.8.0-openjdk
  handlers: ❹
    - name: restart web service
      ansible.builtin.service:
        name: httpd
        state: restarted
  tasks: ❺
    - name: Ensure apache is at the latest version
      ansible.builtin.yum:
        name: httpd
        state: latest
      tags: ['installing'] ❻
```

```
        register: command_output ❼
      - name: Print to console
        ansible.builtin.debug: ❽
          msg: >
   '{{command_output.stdout}}' Remember user: '{{username}}'
   and password: '{{password}}'
      - name: template configuration file
        ansible.builtin.template: ❾
          src: httpd.j2.conf
          dest: /etc/httpd.conf
      - name: restart everything
        ansible.builtin.command: echo "this task will restart the web services"
        notify: "restart web services" ❿
      - name: Create 'books' database user with name 'alex' and password 'alex'.
        mongodb_user: ⓫
          database: books
          name: alex
          password: alex
          state: present
```

❶ Options that affect the current play. Specifically, executing each task within the play as the `root` user.

❷ Defines variables to use in the play.

❸ Registers a role that installs Java within the declared hosts.

❹ Defines handlers executed when they are notified.

❺ Lists tasks using the fully qualified collection name (FQCN) (`ansible.builtin`).

❻ Applies tags to categorize related tasks.

❼ Captures the output from task execution and stores it in a variable (`command_output`).

❽ Prints statements during execution. Variables are set between `{{}}`.

❾ Processes Jinja2 templates and copies output to the location defined by the `dest` property.

❿ Triggers the `restart web service` handler.

⓫ Uses the short name of `mongodb_user` module as the MongoDB collection is imported to add a MongoDB user to the database.

This complete playbook has most of the sections that we would expect in a playbook. Even though we haven't explained all of the components in detail, you can identify each section and its purpose.

We will explore each of the sections in further detail as we go along. But, for the purpose of this chapter, we'll provide a general overview so that you will understand why a playbook is a fundamental component of Ansible.

Variables

Variables let you define dynamic parameters that you can use in playbooks, and take the form of `<key>:<value>` pairs. They can be passed in at runtime on the command line to either set or override the value.

For example, to override the password variable value as shown in the previous playbook, you could run `ansible-playbook` with the `--extra-vars/-e` option:

```
ansible-playbook -i inventory playbook.yaml --extra-vars "password=Gavina"
```

The following chapters will cover variables in further detail, including where and how they can be used. Variables can be set several different ways, including passed as input from the command line, but also from a task output as described in this section.

Roles

As you develop more and more playbooks, you will notice that patterns begin to emerge where steps might be repetitive.

Ansible *roles* let you reuse and share Ansible code, so you (or anyone in your team or the Ansible community) could write the code once and reuse it across multiple playbooks. For example, a role could be created to install PostgreSQL and reuse it in all tasks of all projects when a PostgreSQL database is required. Roles defined within a `roles` section of a playbook are executed before any other tasks in a play. The included roles run in the order they are defined.

In the playbook defined in "An Example Playbook Structure" on page 40, `geerling guy.java` would be executed first against all hosts, and then the rest of the defined tasks. You'll learn more in Chapter 8 about roles, their structure, and how to change when they are executed.

Handlers

Ansible offers *handlers* as a method for executing operations when changes occur; for example, restarting a service when a task changes a configuration file but not when no changes are made. In summary, handlers are tasks that only run when they are triggered.

Handlers are defined in the `handlers` section of a playbook, and by default, they are triggered by their name using the `notify` keyword in the task. In the playbook defined within the "Playbook Structure" section, the task `restart everything` would trigger the defined handler. You will learn more about handlers in Chapter 5.

Tasks

Tasks are invocations of Ansible modules, and the basics have already been introduced. However, in this chapter, you may have noticed a few directives appearing in some of the examples, including `tags` and `register`, as well as the use of the fully qualified name of the module. For example, the `yum` module was defined:

```
- name: Ensure apache is at the latest version
  ansible.builtin.yum:
    name: httpd
    state: latest
```

The fully qualified collection name (FQCN) is the namespace where the module is stored (typically the collection name) separated by periods (`.`), followed by the module name. In the previous snippet, the namespace is `ansible.builtin` and the module name is `yum`.

You do not need to use FQCNs with `ansible.builtin`, and many other collections, because Ansible will resolve the short names to a collection name automatically. Here is the equivalent way to define the module within a task:

```
- name: Ensure apache is at the latest version
  ansible.builtin.yum:
    name: httpd
    state: latest
```

Although the short name form creates a more compact playbook, our advice is to use the FQCN version of the module. Hence, you always know exactly which module you are using as it should avoid any conflicts with modules with the same name in different collections.

Includes and imports. Tasks can also be defined in a separate YAML file and *included* (or *imported*) in the tasks section using the `include_tasks` or `import_tasks` module.

The following snippet shows an example of including tasks defined in an external YAML file:

```
tasks:
  - ansible.builtin.include_tasks: db.yml ❶
```

❶ Content of *db.yml* is included in the `tasks` section

It's important to have an understanding of the differences between importing and including externally sourced content. In summary, `import_tasks` occur at parsing time, so they are not dynamic; meanwhile, `include_tasks` happen at runtime when the playbook is executed.

Imports add the tasks from the file into the playbook, and attributes, like `tags` and `when`, are copied to every imported task. Moreover, when using variables for the target file or role name, you cannot use variables from inventory sources (host/group vars, etc.). Loops are not valid either.

On the other hand, includes are processed during runtime at the point where that task is encountered. This implies you can use variables or loops. Included tasks are similar to handlers—they may or may not run, depending on the results of other tasks in the top-level playbook.

Blocks. Tasks can be grouped into *blocks*. You can think of blocks as a way of inheriting directives among multiple tasks. For example, a block with a privilege escalation is evaluated before Ansible runs each of the three tasks in the block, not at the block level.

```
tasks:
  - name: Install, configure, and start Apache
    become: true ❶
    become_user: root
    block: ❷
      - name: Install httpd and memcached
        ansible.builtin.yum:
          name:
          - httpd
          state: present

      - name: Configure
          ...

      - name: Start service bar and enable it
        ansible.builtin.service:
          name: bar
          state: started
          enabled: True
```

❶ Defines privilege escalation at the block level

❷ Registers blocks inheriting the privilege escalation

Tags

All tasks defined in a playbook are executed by default. Still, in the case of large playbooks, it may be desirable to execute certain parts of the playbook instead of its entirety. For example, you can run specific testing tasks periodically to ensure that the application is running as expected.

Ansible offers *tags* as a way to filter which tasks are executed or which should be skipped. In the previous example, the first task contains a tag named `installing`:

```
tasks:
  - name: Ensure apache is at the latest version
    ansible.builtin.yum:
      name: httpd
      state: latest
    tags: ['installing']
  ...
```

To execute only tasks tagged with the `installing` tag, use the `--tags` option:

```
ansible-playbook playbook.yaml --tags "installing"
```

To execute all tasks except those tagged with `installing`, use the `--skip-tags` option:

```
ansible-playbook playbook.yaml --skip-tags "installing"
```

The `--tags` and `--skip-tags` arguments support a comma-separated list to specify multiple tags.

There are two special arguments for these parameters; the first is `tagged`, which is used for executing all tasks with at least one tag. The second argument is `untagged`, which is used for executing all tasks with no tags.

You can apply tags individually in each task or apply them globally to all tasks defined in a file:

```
tasks:
  - ansible.builtin.include_tasks: db.yml
    tags: db ❶
```

❶ The db tag applies to all tasks defined in *db.yml.*

The same applies to `import_tasks`.

If you want to apply the same tag or tags to multiple tasks without adding the tag to every task, you can define the tags at the level of your *play* or *block*.

For example, you can define tags in a block, as shown in the following snippet:

```
- name: ntp tasks
  tags: ntp
  block:
```

```
- name: Install ntp
  ansible.builtin.yum:
    name: ntp
    state: present
...
```

And in a similar way at the play level:

```
- hosts: all
  tags: play1
  tasks:
    ...
- hosts: db
  tags: play2
  tasks:
    ...
```

Ansible reserves two tag names: `always` and `never`. The `always` tag runs the task or play unless you specifically skip it (`--skip-tags always`). On the other hand, `never` will skip the task or play unless you specifically request it (`--tags never`).

Tags are a relevant feature provided by Ansible for managing playbook executions when they contain a considerable amount of tasks.

Register

Every time Ansible runs a task, some form of output is generated, for example, the start/end date time of the command, the output of the command, the duration time of the command, the return code, if it failed or not, and so on. These output parameters depend on the executed module, some provide brief information about the execution, while others provide more extensive information.

The output is represented in JSON format and, depending on the command, will generate more or fewer fields.

In the following snippet, the output of the `dnf` command is shown:

```
{
    "ansible_facts": {
        "discovered_interpreter_python": "/usr/bin/python3"
    },
    "changed": true,
    "msg": "",
    "rc": 0,
    "stdout": "...",
    "results": [
        "Installed: procps-ng-3.3.17-6.fc37.2.x86_64"
    ]
}
```

In certain situations, you might want to extract some information from the output of a task to either print it in the console (in debugging situations) or use it in other subsequent sections.

To capture the output of a task and store its content into an Ansible variable, use the `register` keyword. Previously, we stored the output of the `yum` command into a variable named `command_output`:

```
tasks:
  - name: Ensure apache is at the latest version
    ansible.builtin.yum:
      name: httpd
      state: latest
    tags: ['installing']
    register: command_output ❶
```

❶ Registers task output in JSON format

You can access the individual fields using dot notation or the Python dictionary.

For example, to access the `rc` field, both of the following forms are valid:

```
- name: Shows the exit code
  ansible.builtin.debug:
    msg: "{{ command_output.rc }}"

- name: Shows the exit code
  ansible.builtin.debug:
    msg: "{{ command_output['rc'] }}"
```

Collections

Collections are a distribution format for Ansible content (playbooks, roles, modules, and so on), so you can reuse them in playbooks instead of repeating them across multiple playbooks. For example, in the initial example of this section, you used the MongoDB collection to deploy a MongoDB database.

Using the collections approach, you do not need to write a big play with authentication logic for MongoDB logic in every playbook you require; instead, you import the collection and set the minimal required attributes.

While we have yet to show you how to create, share, and install Ansible collections, these concepts are reserved for Chapter 8.

What's important in terms of playbook structure is that you can use the `collections` keyword to avoid having to specify the fully qualified name of the module. For example, the task `mongodb_user` from the sample playbook at the beginning of this chapter contains the short name because the MongoDB namespace was imported:

```
collections:
  - community.mongodb
```

If the collection section was not defined, the module name in the task would need to be specified as `community.mongodb.mongodb_user`. You can think of the `collections` section as similar to the `import` section in Java.

Now that we understand the key sections of an Ansible Playbook, let's create a simple playbook showing some of the concepts explained in this section.

Running Your First Playbook

The previous section introduced Ansible Playbooks, covering the most common parts you might encounter or need, such as variables, tasks, handlers, or reusing tasks with includes and imports. You will get more proficient as you work your way through this book. You'll see a set of different examples and situations you may encounter when using Ansible.

In this section, you'll run your first playbook. It's an easy-to-follow playbook showing how to install the nginx web server, configure it, deploy a simple HTML page, test the deployment, and finally, configure the firewall to allow requests to reach the web page.

Environment

To execute the playbook, a user with root privileges is required.

If you already have a Fedora server running, you can skip this step.

For this example, we've provided a preconfigured Fedora VirtualBox image with username `alex` and password `alex` with root privileges. You can download the Fedora image (*https://oreil.ly/hwImS*) and adapt the network configuration to your use case.

Open VirtualBox and import the image with the Bridge network so you can access it from the host machine. Start the Fedora virtual machine by clicking Start, as shown in Figure 3-2.

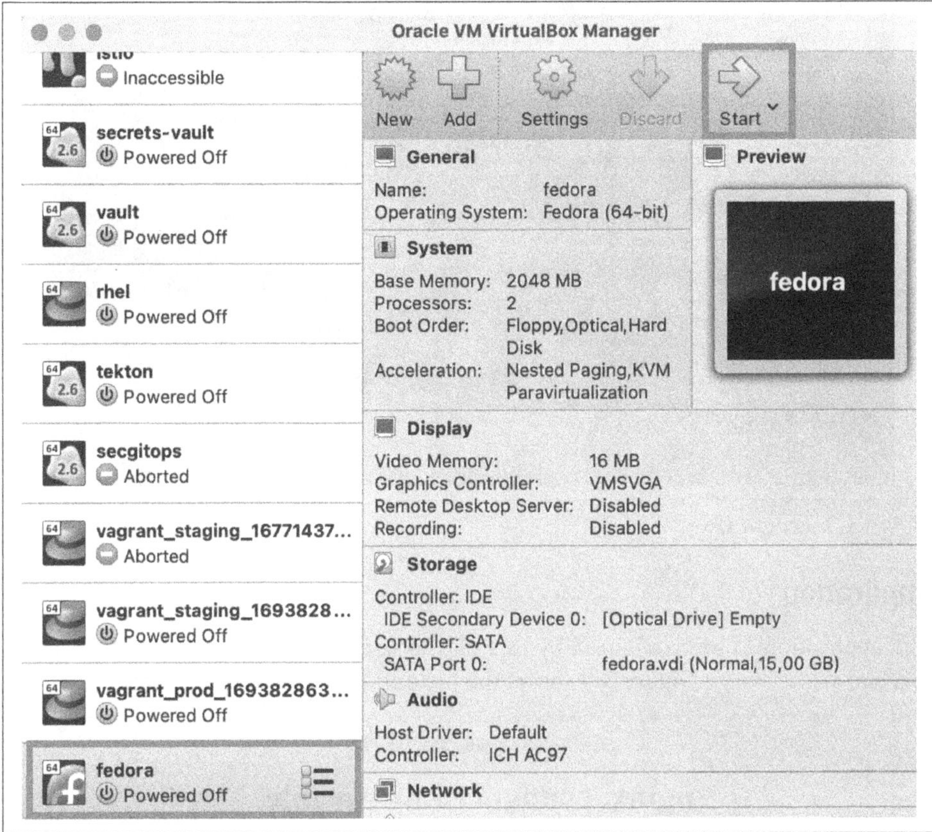

Figure 3-2. VirtualBox menu

When the system is up and running, log in using the user/password `alex`, and execute the `ifconfig` command to get the assigned IP. Figure 3-3 shows the output of the command. In this case, the IP to access the server from the host machine is `192.168.1.115`, and this value needs to be specified in the inventory file.

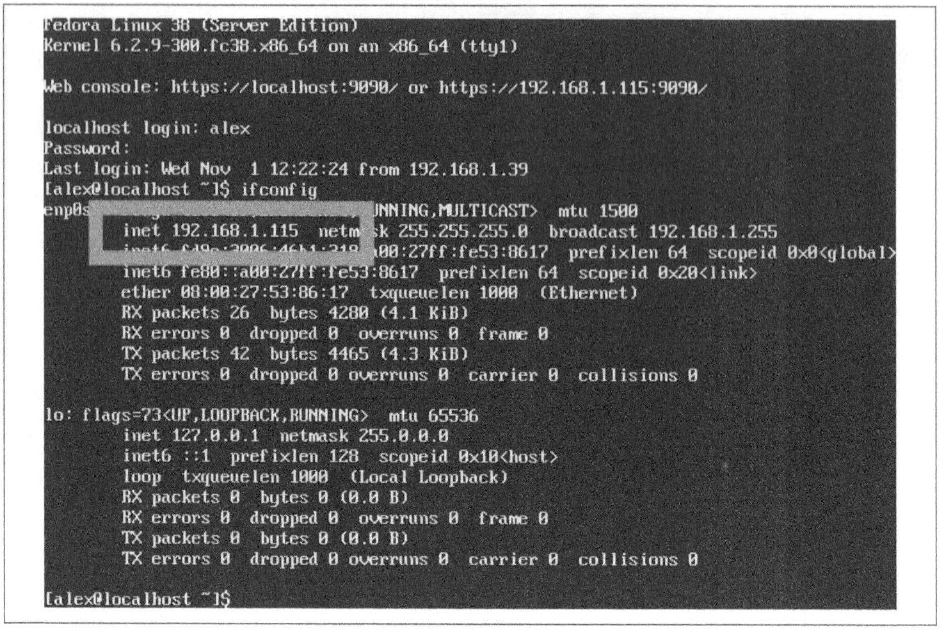

```
Fedora Linux 38 (Server Edition)
Kernel 6.2.9-300.fc38.x86_64 on an x86_64 (tty1)

Web console: https://localhost:9090/ or https://192.168.1.115:9090/

localhost login: alex
Password:
Last login: Wed Nov  1 12:22:24 from 192.168.1.39
[alex@localhost ~]$ ifconfig
enp0s[illegible]UNNING,MULTICAST>  mtu 1500
        inet 192.168.1.115  netm[illegible]sk 255.255.255.0  broadcast 192.168.1.255
        [illegible]a00:27ff:fe53:8617  prefixlen 64  scopeid 0x0<global>
        inet6 fe80::a00:27ff:fe53:8617  prefixlen 64  scopeid 0x20<link>
        ether 08:00:27:53:86:17  txqueuelen 1000  (Ethernet)
        RX packets 26  bytes 4280 (4.1 KiB)
        RX errors 0  dropped 0  overruns 0  frame 0
        TX packets 42  bytes 4465 (4.3 KiB)
        TX errors 0  dropped 0 overruns 0  carrier 0  collisions 0

lo: flags=73<UP,LOOPBACK,RUNNING>  mtu 65536
        inet 127.0.0.1  netmask 255.0.0.0
        inet6 ::1  prefixlen 128  scopeid 0x10<host>
        loop  txqueuelen 1000  (Local Loopback)
        RX packets 0  bytes 0 (0.0 B)
        RX errors 0  dropped 0  overruns 0  frame 0
        TX packets 0  bytes 0 (0.0 B)
        TX errors 0  dropped 0 overruns 0  carrier 0  collisions 0

[alex@localhost ~]$
```

Figure 3-3. Fedora IP

Application

The application to be configured by this playbook is a simple web page (*index.html*) that shows a message. Figure 3-4 shows the the output of the rendered page.

← → C ▲ Not Secure | 192.168.1.115

nginx, configured by Ansible

If you can see this, Ansible successfully installed nginx.

Figure 3-4. ngnix welcome page

The first step before deploying the application is to create the *index.html* file and the nginx configuration file. In a new directory, create the *index.html* file with the following content:

```
<html>
  <head>
    <title>Welcome to ansible</title>
  </head>
  <body>
  <h1>nginx, configured by Ansible</h1>
  <p>If you can see this, Ansible successfully installed nginx.</p>
```

```
    </body>
</html>
```

Then create the *nginx.conf* file with nginx configuration properties:

```
server {
        listen 80 default_server;
        listen [::]:80 default_server ipv6only=on;

        root /usr/share/nginx/html;
        index index.html index.htm;

        server_name localhost;

        location / {
                try_files $uri $uri/ =404;
        }
}
```

Now you can develop the Ansible automation content for deploying the application.

Creating the Inventory and Playbook Files

The first file to create is the inventory file. As we mentioned earlier, the inventory file contains, among other things, the location of the machines to apply Ansible tasks. In this case, it's a simple inventory file with a single machine defined and the user and password to access the instance over the SSH protocol. In Chapter 4, we'll explore inventory files in further detail.

In the same directory where the files were created in the previous section, create the inventory file called *inventory* with the following content:

```
[node1]
192.168.1.115 ansible_user=alex ansible_ssh_pass=alex
```

The group is named `node1`. Change the IP with the address of your machine as obtained earlier. `ansible_user` and `ansible_ssh_pass` are variables set in the inventory and are used during the SSH connection.

It is bad practice to have passwords in clear text. For the sake of simplification, we are doing it this way. Later in the book we'll show you how to fix this.

Last, create the playbook file that performs the following actions:

- Installs nginx
- Configures nginx

- Copies the HTML file to the appropriate directory to publish the web page
- Restarts nginx to apply the configuration changes
- Tests that the web page is correctly published
- Configures the firewall

Create the *playbook.yaml* file with the following content:

```
- name: Configure nginx
  hosts: all
  become: true ❶

  tasks:
    - name: install nginx
      ansible.builtin.dnf: ❷
        name: nginx

    - name: install firewalld
      dnf:
        name: firewalld

    - name: copy nginx config file
      ansible.builtin.copy: ❸
        src: nginx.conf
        dest: /etc/nginx/conf.d/localhost.conf

    - name: copy index.html
      ansible.builtin.copy:
        src: index.html
        dest: /usr/share/nginx/html/index.html
        mode: 0644
      tags: ['deploy'] ❹

    - name: restart nginx
      ansible.builtin.service:
        name: nginx
        state: restarted
      tags: ['deploy']

    - name: Check status 200 and fail if incorrect page contents
      ansible.builtin.uri: ❺
        url: http://localhost/index.html
        return_content: yes
      register: response
      tags: ['deploy']

    - name: Print result
      ansible.builtin.debug:
        var: response.content
      tags: ['deploy', 'test']
```

```
- name: permit traffic in default zone for http service
  ansible.posix.firewalld: ❻
    service: http
    permanent: true
    state: enabled

- name: restart firewalld
  ansible.builtin.service:
    name=firewalld
    state=restarted
```

❶ Privilege escalation.

❷ Installs nginx using the `dnf` tool.

❸ Copies a file from the control machine to the managed node.

❹ Creates a tag for executing only an update of the web page content.

❺ Uses the `uri` module to perform an invocation to the web server, storing the output into the `response` variable.

❻ Configures the firewall to permit traffic for the HTTP port.

The final step is executing this playbook with the `ansible-playbook` tool. In the terminal window, run the following command:

```
ansible-playbook -i inventory -K  playbook.yaml
```

When Ansible asks you for the `become` password, specify `alex` as the password so the user becomes root.

If you get an error like:

```
fatal: [192.168.0.17]: FAILED! => {"msg": "Using a SSH
password instead of a key is not possible because Host
Key checking is enabled and sshpass does not support this.
Please add this host's fingerprint to your known_hosts
file to manage this host."}
```

create a file in the same directory named *ansible.cfg* with the following content:

```
[defaults]
host_key_checking = false
```

The output of the command is shown in the snippet:

```
BECOME password:
```

```
PLAY [Configure nginx] *****

TASK [Gathering Facts] ****
ok: [192.168.1.115]

TASK [install nginx] ****
changed: [192.168.1.115]

TASK [copy nginx config file] ****
ok: [192.168.1.115]

TASK [copy index.html] ****
changed: [192.168.1.115]

TASK [restart nginx] ****
changed: [192.168.1.115]

TASK [Check status 200 and fail if incorrect page contents] ***
ok: [192.168.1.115]

TASK [Print result] ****
ok: [192.168.1.115] => {
    "response.content": "<html>\n  <head>\n
    <title>Welcome to ansible</title>\n  </head>\n
    <body>\n  <h1>nginx, configured by Ansible</h1>\n
    <p>If you can see this, Ansible successfully installed nginx.</p>\n\n
    </body>\n</html>\n"
}

TASK [permit traffic in default zone for https service] ****
ok: [192.168.1.115]

TASK [restart firewalld] ****
changed: [192.168.1.115]

PLAY RECAP ****
192.168.1.115              : ok=9    changed=4    unreachable=0    failed=0
  skipped=0
                                rescued=0    ignored=0
```

Open your browser and access the web page at the IP address of the server.

Conclusion

At this point, you should have a good overview of the basics of Ansible, the parts that compose it, how it works, and how it can be executed. In the following chapters, we'll explore the details of the elements we have introduced in these initial chapters.

CHAPTER 4

Variables and Host Management

Thus far, we have explored several key Ansible concepts: the inventory to define the managed hosts, the playbook to register the actions to execute against the managed hosts, and the variables or modules.

In this chapter, you'll expand your knowledge and focus in on variables and how they are involved in host management, and in particular, the inventory. We will touch upon the differences between static and dynamic inventories, how to create and organize a hierarchy of hosts into groups, and how to define specific variables per host.

You will learn about several methods by which variables can be defined and the implications that are associated with each choice. You will also see how they are applied on host management operations. Finally, we will discuss how and where variables can be overridden, and how to protect variables that contain sensitive data.

Ansible Facts

In most cases, Ansible communicates with a remote host and performs some form of automation (installing dependencies, copying files, configuring users, etc.). These hosts contain attributes that might be useful within automation activities, such as in a task.

The types of information that are associated with a host include the hardware architecture, current time, devices, network information, kernel version, mounted filesystems, and memory. This information is known in Ansible as *Ansible facts*.

Ansible sets these facts as variables, which enables you to use them as you see fit. For example, logic could be applied to configure the system based on the amount of memory installed within the host, or setting a configuration file based on networking details, such as an IP address.

Facts are *eager variables*, meaning all are gathered automatically at the beginning of each play. This impacts the startup performance of any playbook, since the first step requires communicating and gathering all of the facts associated with a host. We'll see later how to opt out of gathering.

Let's start by using the Ansible CLI tool to retrieve and print all facts from a host.

Setup Module

The `setup` Ansible module enables the retrieval of facts from a host. To view the facts of the server started in Chapter 3, run the following command from within the terminal:

```
ansible all -i inventory -m ansible.builtin.setup

"ansible_facts": {
    "ansible_all_ipv4_addresses": [
        "192.168.1.115"
    ],
    "ansible_all_ipv6_addresses": [
         "fd9c:3006:46b1:318:a00:27ff:fe53:8617",
         "fe80::a00:27ff:fe53:8617"
        ],
    "ansible_apparmor": {
        "status": "disabled"
    },
    "ansible_architecture": "x86_64",
    "ansible_bios_date": "12/01/2006",
    "ansible_bios_vendor": "innotek GmbH",
    "ansible_bios_version": "VirtualBox",
...
    "ansible_nodename": "localhost.localdomain",
    "ansible_os_family": "RedHat",
    "ansible_pkg_mgr": "dnf",
...
    "ansible_selinux": {
        "config_mode": "enforcing",
        "mode": "enforcing",
        "policyvers": 33,
        "status": "enabled",
        "type": "targeted"
    }
...
```

Fact Variables

Facts are stored within a variable named `ansible_facts`, a dictionary-like structure that can be accessed using brackets (`[`, `]`), with the property's name as the key, or by using dot notation (`.`), where each nested value is separated by a period.

We can use the same host from Chapter 3 to create a simple task to print all the facts in an Ansible playbook. Use the `debug` module to print the retrieved facts to the terminal.

Create a new playbook file named *playbook-facts.yaml* with the following content:

```
- name: Gather Ansible facts
  hosts: all
  become: true

  tasks:
  - name: Print all available facts
    ansible.builtin.debug:
      var: ansible_facts ❶
```

❶ Prints to console the value of the variable

In the terminal window, run the following command:

```
ansible-playbook -i inventory -K  playbook-facts.yaml
```

The output is a JSON document with all the facts and their values.

You can reference the output in a Jinja template (more about this in Chapter 6) or playbook and get a property value individually. This is especially useful within a Jinja template or in conditionals/loops. For example, the memory limits of the application can be configured depending on the available physical memory of the instance, or specific tasks can be executed depending on the particular Linux distribution installed.

To reference the OS family, use `{{ ansible_facts['os_family'] }}`, or to access the SELinux configuration, use the array form `{{ansible_facts['selinux']['configmode']}}`. You can also access certain Ansible facts as top-level variables with the `ansible_` prefix; for example, you can directly access the node name by using the `ansible_nodename` variable.

Disabling Gathering Facts

Gathering facts does impact the overall execution time, especially when there are many nodes for which information needs to be gathered.

If you are not using any information that would originate from facts, you can speed up the startup process by turning off this step by setting the `gather_facts` property to `false`, as shown:

```
- hosts: whatever
  gather_facts: false
```

In the next section, we'll review a key concept in Ansible that provides you the ability to change values at execution time—variables.

Ansible Variables

Similar to any programming language, Ansible provides the concept of variables. A variable lets you change a common function's behavior by providing a different value as an input parameter at runtime.

There are a ton of use cases where variables are helpful. Let's start with a simple example: a task copying a file from the local disk to a disk on the remote host where the location of the disk is configured using a variable.

Simple, List, and Dictionary Variables

A variable name can only include letters, numbers, and underscores, for example, `foo` or `bar`. There are also limitations to the names associated with variables. Python keywords or playbook keywords are not valid variable names (such as `async`, `lambda`, or `environment`). A variable name cannot begin with a number, like `13foo` or `12`, for example.

The value of a variable can be expressed as a string, boolean, or number in its simple form. It can also be a list or dictionary. Let's explore several examples where different types of variables are used.

Simple variables

A simple variable contains only the name of the variable with its value:

```
remote_path: /etc/nginx/conf.d
```

To reference a simple variable, use Jinja2 syntax, which uses double curly braces (`{{var}}`):

```
ansible.builtin.copy:
  src: nginx.conf
  dest: '{{remote_path}}/localhost.conf' ❶
```

❶ Variable replaced at runtime

The value part of the dest property is quoted because of a restriction of the YAML format. If a value of a YAML property starts with the variable format ({{}}), the YAML parser is not able to determine the type of the property (dest in the previous example) and throws an error. To avoid this issue, the expression needs to be quoted explicitly to instruct the parser that the value is a string and not the start of a YAML dictionary.

Ansible accepts a broad range of values for boolean variables: true/false, 1/0, yes/no, True/False, t/f, y/n, or on/off.

List variables

A list variable combines a variable name with multiple values. The values are defined either as an itemized list or in square bracket [] form, separated with commas:

```
configFiles:
  - localhost.conf
  - extra.conf
```

Or, the equivalent in bracket form:

```
configFiles: ['localhost.conf', 'extra.conf']
```

To reference an item within a list variable, specify the location as a 0-based index within the variable:

```
ansible.builtin.copy:
  src: nginx.conf
  dest: '{{remote_path}}/{{configFiles[0]}}' ❶
```

❶ The destination file is *localhost.conf*.

Dictionary variables

A dictionary stores the data in key-value pairs, like the structure of a Map included in many programming languages. The values are defined using YAML dictionaries:

```
configFiles:
  local: localhost.conf ❶ ❷
  extra: extra.conf
```

❶ The key is local.

❷ The value is localhost.conf.

To reference a dictionary entry, two options are available: bracket notation (var[key]) or dot notation (var.key). For example, to access the local value, both of the following options are valid:

```
{{configFiles['local']}}
```

```
{{configFiles.local}}
```

In both cases, the result will be localhost.conf.

We recommend you always use bracket notation because some keys might collide with attributes and methods of Python dictionaries in dot notation, or the keys themselves could include a period, which would result in undesirable outcomes.

Setting Variable Values

So far, you have seen how to define variables and refer to them in Ansible playbooks, but where can you set the values of variables?

In Ansible, there are multiple places to define variables, like playbooks, roles, inventories, and the command-line tools. Let's see some examples of the different places where variables can be set.

Playbooks

You can define variables in a playbook by setting them in the vars section. Let's define a variable in a playbook named msg_name:

```
- hosts: webservers
  vars:
    msg_name: Hello World Alexandra ❶
```

❶ This variable definition is valid within the play.

To see variables in action, let's create a simple playbook file that prints the variable to the managed/remote host using the echo command, captures the command output into a registered variable, and prints the result using the debug module.

You can run the following example against any of the machines created in the previous chapters. Remember to configure the inventory file correctly.

Create a new playbook file with the following content:

```
- name: Echoing Vars
  hosts: all
  vars:
    msg_name: Alexandra ❶
  tasks:
```

```
    - name: Echo var
      ansible.builtin.command: /bin/echo "Hello World {{msg_name}}" ❷
      register: response ❸
    - name: Print result
      ansible.builtin.debug:
        var: response ❹
```

❶ Defines the value of the variable

❷ Uses the variable as an argument of the echo command

❸ Captures the command output

❹ Prints the variable value to the control node

Run the playbook and observe the output in a terminal:

```
ansible-playbook -i inventory playbook-vars.yaml

...
TASK [Echo var] ****
changed: [192.168.0.17]

TASK [Print result] *****
ok: [192.168.0.17] => {
    "response": {
        "changed": true,
        "cmd": [
            "/bin/echo",
            "Hello World Alexandra" ❶
        ],
        "delta": "0:00:00.005838",
        "end": "2023-12-28 14:14:42.167370",
        "failed": false,
        "msg": "",
        "rc": 0,
        "start": "2023-12-28 14:14:42.161532",
        "stderr": "",
        "stderr_lines": [],
        "stdout": "Hello World Alexandra",
        "stdout_lines": [
            "Hello World Alexandra"
        ]
    }
}

PLAY RECAP ****
192.168.0.17
```

❶ The command (executed appropriately) resolved the variable value

Files

Another option is to set variables in an external YAML-formatted file. By externalizing the variables outside the playbook itself, it enables populating the file with different variables for the specific situation or environment. In addition, it also avoids including sensitive data within the playbook. The playbook user is responsible for ensuring the file with the correct variable values has been created and is present.

Let's modify the previous example to set the variable within an external file instead of embedded within the playbook. Create a new file named *external_vars.yaml* with the following content:

```
msg_name: Anna
```

Modify the playbook to load variables from the file using the `vars_files` section to specify the file location instead of `vars`:

```
- name: Echoing Vars
  hosts: all
  vars_files: ❶
    - external_vars.yaml ❷
  tasks:
```

❶ List of files with variables declarations

❷ Location of the file specified either as an absolute path or relative to the current playbook

If you run the previous playbook, the variable value changed to `Anna`.

Besides defining variables in external files, Ansible lets you define variables in special files based on specific hosts or groups of hosts:

host_vars
: A folder relative to the inventory file or playbook file, which references each specific device defined in the inventory. The YAML files with the variables definitions must be named exactly as the hosts in the inventory.

group_vars
: A folder relative to the inventory file or the playbook file, which references groups of devices or all devices specified in the inventory. The YAML files with the variables definitions must be named exactly as the groups in the inventory, or `all` if they affect all groups.

Set up the following inventory file:

```
[therock] ; ❶
db ansible_host=192.168.0.17 ; ❷
web ansible_host=192.168.0.18 ansible_user=alex ansible_ssh_pass=alex
```

```
[barcelona] ; ❸
db2 ansible_host=192.168.0.19 ansible_user=alex ansible_ssh_pass=alex
web2 ansible_host=192.168.0.20 ansible_user=alex ansible_ssh_pass=alex
```

❶ Establishes the group of hosts called `therock` containing two hosts

❷ Aliases the hostname to `db`

❸ Another group of hosts

Let's see how to use *host_vars* and *group_vars*.

host_vars

Create a new directory named *host_vars* in the same directory as the example we're working on in this chapter:

```
mkdir host_vars
```

Inside this directory, create a new file named *db.yml*, which represents the name of the host defined in the inventory, with the following content:

```
ansible_user: alex
ansible_ssh_pass: alex
msg_name: Anna
```

Connection and custom variables are set for the `db` host as the file is placed in *host_vars* and named appropriately with the hostname.

Host variables are specific to hosts, so they are useful when defining variables in small scenarios or for individual machines. Still, in the case of large scenarios with many instances, such as in data centers with multiple locations, *group_vars* might be a better option.

group_vars

Create a new directory named *group_vars* in the same directory as the example we're working on in this chapter.

Inside this directory, create a new file named *therock.yml*, as `therock` is one of the groups that we defined previously within the inventory file, and populate it with the following content:

```
ansible_user: alex
ansible_ssh_pass: alex
msg_name: Natale
```

At this point, all hosts under the `therock` group will use the same variable values.

If you want to apply common variable values to all groups, you can create a file called *all.yml* so that all inventory hosts will use the variable values specified. The final location where you can specify variables is within the inventory. We have actually seen this already in our previous examples, but will provide an overview with further details.

Inventory

Defining variables in inventory files is a good option to have when you need to have the host definitions together with their variables. While the primary use of inventory variables within inventory files is related to connection properties, any other variable can be defined as well.

In the inventory, let's see the different ways how `ansible_user` and `ansible_ssh_pass` variables can be defined.

The first example is per-host definitions. There have already been several examples demonstrating this pattern. The following is a reminder:

```
[therock]
192.168.1.115 ansible_user=alex ansible_ssh_pass=alex ; ❶
```

❶ Sets two variables for this host

Variables can also be applied to an entire group at once:

```
[therock]
192.168.1.115

[therock:vars] ; ❶
ansible_user=alex
ansible_ssh_pass=alex
```

❶ Defines vars for a specific group

The equivalent inventory file in YAML format:

```
therock:
  hosts:
    192.168.1.115:
  vars:
    ansible_user: alex
    ansible_ssh_pass: alex
```

To specify to all hosts/groups, use the `[all:vars]` or `all:` syntax.

Now that we've looked at three locations where you can specify variables, let's see how you can override them at runtime.

Runtime

You can define variables at runtime by passing variables at the command line using the `--extra-vars` (or `-e`) argument. For example, to override the `msg_name` variable from the command line, execute the following command:

```
ansible-playbook -i inventory playbook-vars.yaml --extra-vars="msg_name=Kevin"
```

The `extra-vars` flag allows you to specify multiple parameters. Either the property-based (`"var1=foo var2=bar"`) or YAML format (`'{"var1":"foo","var2":"bar"}'`) is supported.

When defining many variables at runtime, it is useful to define them in a file (JSON or YAML) and refer to it using the `@` symbol, for example, `--extra-vars @some_file.json` or `--extra-vars @some_file.yaml`.

If you want your playbook to prompt the user for a certain input, add a `vars_prompt` section and define the variables the user interactively fills at runtime. This is useful when a human is needed to provide content based on a particular situation or use case.

To let the user define the `msg_name` variable value at runtime, modify the playbook by adding the `vars_prompt` section, as follows:

```
- name: Echoing Vars
  hosts: all
  vars_prompt: ❶
    - name: msg_name ❷
      prompt: What's the name?
      private: false ❸
      default: Ada
  tasks:
    - name: Echo var
      ansible.builtin.command: /bin/echo "Hello World {{msg_name}}"
      register: response
    - name: Print result
      ansible.builtin.debug:
        var: response
```

❶ Section for the prompted `vars`

❷ Name of the prompted `vars`

❸ User input is not hidden

Run the playbook and fill in the prompted variable:

```
ansible-playbook -i inventory playbook-prompt-vars.yaml

Whats the name? [Ada]: Aixa

"response": {
        "changed": true,
        "cmd": [
            "/bin/echo",
            "Hello World Aixa"
        ],
```

For sensitive values, you can hash the entered value so you can use it, for example, with the user module to define a password:

```
vars_prompt:
  - name: password
    prompt: Enter the password
    private: true
    encrypt: sha512_crypt
    confirm: true
    salt_size: 7
```

Variable precedence

Ansible applies variable precedence, so one value might be overridden because of the location where it is defined. The following list details the precedence applied to variables from lowest to highest as noted within the Ansible documentation (*https://oreil.ly/HWBVP*):

1. Role defaults (defined in `role/defaults/main.yml`)
2. Inventory file or script group `vars`
3. Inventory `group_vars/all`
4. Playbook `group_vars/all`
5. Inventory `group_vars/*`
6. Playbook `group_vars/*`
7. Inventory file or script host `vars`
8. Inventory `host_vars/*`
9. Playbook `host_vars/*`
10. Host facts/cached `set_facts`
11. Play `vars`
12. Play `vars_prompt`
13. Play `vars_files`

14. Role `vars` (defined in `role/vars/main.yml`)
15. Block `vars` (only for tasks in the block)
16. Task `vars` (only for the task)
17. `include_vars`
18. `set_facts`/registered vars
19. Role (and `include_role`) params
20. Include params
21. Extra `vars` (for example, `-e "user=my_user"`)(always win precedence)

With a deep understanding of variables, where to define them, and where to use them (a variable can replace any value set in an Ansible file), let's move forward to understand how to manage these variables when they contain sensitive data, like passwords.

Protecting Sensitive Data

Ansible automation routinely requires the use of sensitive values. To keep them secure, they should not be stored or declared in plain text. In addition, if the file is pushed to a Git repository, everyone with access to the repository, or if an attacker gets access to it, could get the secret values.

In the previous section, we created and injected variables for use within playbooks. The examples were simple: a variable was defined in a file in plain-text format, read by Ansible, and injected into the playbook. If we wanted to declare variables that contain sensitive data, like a username and password, we would need to investigate alternate methods for securing the values.

Ansible Vault, a tool included with Ansible, provides a way to encrypt/decrypt and manage sensitive data, such as passwords, certificates, keys, API tokens, etc. Let's showcase how we can update our example to secure sensitive values.

Encrypting Data

Let's create a YAML file named *prod.yaml* with variable definitions, but this time, with encrypted content. Run the following command in the terminal window to start the encryption of variables in interactive mode:

```
ansible-vault create prod.yaml
```

After running the command, the terminal prompts you to enter the password that will be used to encrypt the file where variables are defined. Enter the password `secret`:

```
New Vault password:
Confirm New Vault password:
```

Ansible opens the system editor to allow you to define the values that should be encrypted. In this example, a username and password should be specified. However, you could set anything you need to protect:

```
username: Secret1
password: Secret2
```

When you save the file, Ansible encrypts its content and places the output on disk.

Inspect the generated file to validate that is encrypted and very hard to crack:

```
$ANSIBLE_VAULT;1.1;AES256
66343761653764386535666430306133386536303662373335633638653562373035316632643366
30323561643061653239643037646162316435623566626 50a386336633037666234333430353837
35643966373537323264333461353035623639386562663561363666353938616432656264626164
3332326431306362370a626538636336646530363037346261616631393438353865303934363934
63333830346334623235653565643463326461663839616366333533303436376161626433303765
623133366235636464613836613464386433356565663436663 4
```

The file is now encrypted, which restricts the ability for an attacker to gain access to the values. At this point, the file is safe to publish in the Git repository or be shared with others.

Decrypting

To decrypt this file while running Ansible, use the `--ask-vault-pass` option to set Ansible to ask for the password to decrypt the files.

Given the following playbook:

```
- name: Echoing Vars
  hosts: all
  tasks:
    - name: Echo var
      ansible.builtin.command: >
        /bin/echo "The username is {{username}}
        and the password {{password}}"
      register: response
    - name: Print result
      ansible.builtin.debug:
        var: response
```

Run the following command in the terminal to validate that the variable definitions file is decrypted and values are injected into the playbook:

```
ansible-playbook \
  -i inventory \
  --extra-vars "@prod.yaml" \
  --ask-vault-pass \
  playbook-enc.yaml
```

Ansible prompts you to enter the password to decrypt the file; for this specific case, the password is `secret`. If you chose to utilize a different value for the password when creating the encrypted file, use that value instead.

The output of the playbook shows the content decrypted in the managed host:

```
ok: [db] => {
    "response": {
        "changed": true,
        "cmd": [
            "/bin/echo",
            "The username is Secret and the password Secret"
        ],
        "delta": "0:00:00.008635",
        "end": "2023-12-30 22:12:36.580921",
        "failed": false,
        "msg":"  ",
        "rc": 0,
        "start": "2023-12-30 22:12:36.572286",
        "stderr":"  ",
        "stderr_lines": [],
        "stdout": "The username is Secret and the password Secret",
        "stdout_lines": [
            "The username is Secret and the password Secret"
        ]
    }
}
```

All of these processes occur securely, so only the user managing Ansible automation knows the secret for decrypting the files. Keep in mind that losing the Vault password means losing your data, and you'll need to encrypt it again with a new password.

Any Ansible file, like inventory, templates, or configuration files, can be secured similarly.

Ansible automatically picks up the secrets file if placed in the *host_vars/<host_name>* folder.

In the final section of this chapter, we will look at how to create static and dynamic inventories, along with additional tips and tricks you can use when managing a large number of hosts.

Host Management

The Ansible inventory file defines all the managed hosts and groups of managed hosts for which tasks will be executed. We've already covered the basics of inventories in Chapter 2, along with examples of their use in each chapter, as inventories are a central component of Ansible. So far, the details were purely introductory. This section will explore inventories in further detail and describe how to create inventory files for managing multiple hosts.

Using Ranges

If you have a large number of hosts with similar names, you can add them as a range rather than specifying each instance separately. For example, in the case of five hosts named `db01.example.com` through `db05.example.com`, you could use the following pattern:

```
db[01:05].example.com
```

You can add increments as the third argument as well; for example, `db[01:10:2].example.com`, which will increment by two the range of integers (`db01`, `db03`, ...).

Ansible also supports alphabetic ranges , for example, `db[a:f].example.com`.

Grouping Groups

You can aggregate multiple groups as children under a parent group. This is useful when you have multiple data centers or environments with different hosts (web servers, databases, etc.) and want to control them individually or globally.

Let's look at the following inventory containing no child groups:

```
[tokyo]
db1.example.com
web1.example.com

[denver]
db2.example.com
web2.example.com
```

Using this inventory, you can only easily apply changes to all hosts or hosts under the `tokyo` or `denver` groups. But what if you want to select only *webX* hosts or *dbX* hosts?

One way would be to use a regular expression of host matching, for example, `ansible-playbook -i inventory -l ~web.*\.example\.com playbook.yaml`. It's doable, but working with regular expressions is always complex and challenging to maintain. In addition, any minor error in the expression might result in an unexpected and catastrophic result.

An easy way to structure the inventory is by using groups and subgroups. The previous inventory could be rewritten to the following:

```
[web_tokyo]
web1.example.com

[web_denver]
web2.example.com

[db_tokyo]
db1.example.com

[db_denver]
db2.example.com

[webservers:children] ; ❶
web_tokyo ; ❷
web_denver

[dbservers:children]
db_tokyo
db_denver

[denver:children]
db_denver
web_denver

[tokyo:children]
web_tokyo
db_tokyo
```

❶ The `children` keyword sets the subgroup.

❷ Refers to the group name.

To run a playbook against any defined groups, use the `-l` parameter to limit the execution to a particular set of hosts. For example, to run a playbook to the `tokyo` data center, you can run the following command:

```
ansible-playbook -i inventory_groups -l tokyo playbook.yaml
```

The equivalent in YAML is:

```
web_tokyo:
  hosts:
    web1.example.com

web_denver:
  hosts:
    web2.example.com

db_tokyo:
```

```
    hosts:
      db1.example.com

  db_denver:
    hosts:
      db2.example.com
  tokyo:
    children:
      web_tokyo:
      db_tokyo:

  ....
```

Organizing Inventory in a Directory

Usually, you would define a single inventory file. However, managing a single file gets difficult to maintain when there are multiple hosts, variables, groups, and so on, in use. To simplify this host management challenge, Ansible lets you define a directory that can contain multiple inventory files and will be merged at runtime.

The following *inventory* directory contains multiple inventory files in INI and YAML formats representing different types of hosts:

```
inventory/
  dbs.yml
  web-inventory
  network
```

You can target this inventory by specifying the directory as a parameter of the `-i` argument using the `ansible` or `ansible-playbook` command-line interfaces:

```
ansible-playbook playbook.yml -i inventory
```

Ansible loads inventory in ASCII order according to the filenames. If you define parent groups in one file or directory and child groups in other files or directories, the files that define the child groups must be loaded first. You can control the load order by adding prefixes to the files, like `01-dbs.yml`, `02-web-inventory`, etc.

Dynamic Inventories

So far, the inventories that we have been using have consisted of static files. The hosts are defined and they remain the same group of hosts with no major changes over time. This approach works when the infrastructure does not change. However, if the states of hosts are constantly changing, such as spinning up and shutting down in response to business demands, the static inventory solutions described thus far will not serve your needs.

You may need to track hosts from multiple sources more dynamically so that hosts are added or removed from the inventory automatically. Ansible provides inventory plug-ins to connect to sources and that enable the retrieval of hosts representing the current state of the environment. Prime examples where dynamic inventories shine can include executing against an AWS EC2 account where you need to retrieve all machines, or retrieve machines from other sources of truth, such as from LDAP, a Cobbler server, or Zabbix.

To use an inventory plug-in, you must provide an inventory source. This is usually a file containing host information or a YAML configuration file with options for the plug-in. Each plug-in has its configuration properties and schema, configuration files to create, and dependencies to install.

There are a lot of plug-ins developed and bundled in Ansible. To see the list of available plug-ins, use the `ansible-doc` tool. Use the `-t` parameter to limit the results to `inventory` types:

```
ansible-doc -t inventory -l

amazon.aws.aws_ec2                      EC2 inventory source
amazon.aws.aws_rds                      RDS instance inventory source
ansible.builtin.advanced_host_list  Parses a 'host list' with ranges
ansible.builtin.auto                    Loads and executes an inventory plugin
specified
                                        in a YAML config
ansible.builtin.constructed             Uses Jinja2 to construct vars and groups
                                        based on existing inventory
ansible.builtin.generator               Uses Jinja2 to construct hosts and groups
from patterns
...
```

Use the command `ansible-doc -t inventory <plugin name>` to see plug-in-specific documentation and examples:

```
ansible-doc -t inventory ansible.builtin.advanced_host_list

> ANSIBLE.BUILTIN.ADVANCED_HOST_LIST    (/usr/local/lib/python3.10/
site-packages/ansible/plugins/inventory/advanced_host_list.py)

        Parses a host list string as a comma-separated value of hosts and
        supports host ranges. This plugin only applies to inventory sources
        that are not paths and contain at least one comma.

ADDED IN: version 2.4 of ansible-core

....
```

Ansible's Docker Inventory Plug-In

To understand how dynamic inventories work, use the Ansible Docker inventory plug-in to connect to a Docker host and get the running containers as inventory items.

To execute this example, have a Docker host running on your local machine.

The plug-in to dynamically retrieve containers running in a Docker host is located in the `community.docker` collection called `community.docker.docker_containers`. Run the following command to get information about the plug-in, supported parameters, and examples:

```
ansible-doc -t inventory community.docker.docker_containers

 COMMUNITY.DOCKER.DOCKER_CONTAINERS     (/Users/asotobu/.ansible/collections/
 ansible_collections/community/docker/plugins/inventory/docker_containers.py)

        Reads inventories from the Docker API. Uses a YAML configuration file
        that ends with 'docker.[yml|yaml]'.

EXAMPLES

 Minimal example using local Docker daemon
plugin: community.docker.docker_containers
docker_host: unix://var/run/docker.sock
...
```

First, the results mention the configuration filename pattern ending in *docker* and the extension. Then, the results explain all the configuration parameters to set in the file. Finally, there are some examples to help you understand how to create the file.

To get started, install the Docker collection by running the following command:

```
ansible-galaxy collection install community.docker
```

With the collection installed, start a container in the Docker host:

```
docker run -it --rm --name test redhat/ubi8
```

The final step is to configure the dynamic inventory plug-in. Create a file named *main_docker.yaml* with the following content:

```
plugin: community.docker.docker_containers ❶
docker_host: unix://var/run/docker.sock ❷
connection_type: docker-cli ❸
```

❶ Configures the plug-in to use

❷ Sets the Docker host location

❸ Configures the plug-in to use the `docker-cli` tool instead of the Docker API

Run the `ansible-inventory` command to get the devices present in the Ansible inventory:

```
ansible-inventory -i main_docker.yaml --graph

@all:
  |--@ungrouped:
  |  |--test ❶
```

❶ Test container is present as a host in the inventory

Stopping the running container and listing the hosts in the inventory again will result in an empty list of hosts:

```
docker stop test
```

Conclusion

With a good understanding of variables and host management, you can move on to the next chapter to learn about changing the execution flow of Ansible playbooks.

CHAPTER 5

Flow Control

Thus far, you've gotten most of the knowledge needed to operate Ansible correctly. You know how to define tasks, manage hosts, and execute tasks.

In the rest of the book, you'll learn Ansible concepts that will enable you to create Ansible playbooks that are more compact, reusable, and readable. In this chapter, we'll focus on how to change the flow of the execution of a task depending on certain situations, like an error, a condition, or executing a task multiple times.

Loops

In some cases, you might want to execute the same task with minor variations multiple times in the same play or retry a failing task various times to self-correct any temporary errors. Examples of loops include:

- Copying multiple files
- Creating users
- Installing multiple tools
- Executing the same command multiple times with different arguments

Similar to any programming language, there are special keywords to identify loops.

Using Loops

In Ansible, you can iterate over any variable of type list, a list of hashes, or a dictionary. Some of these variables can be explicitly created (e.g., a list of programs to install), but others are implicit, like the inventory hosts list. In each iteration, Ansible will set the current value in a variable named `item`.

Let's start with a simple example. Suppose you need to install Java 17 and Apache Maven into a host. With what you've learned so far in this book about Ansible, you could write something like:

```
tasks:
  - name: Install Java 17
    ansible.builtin.dnf:
      name: java-17-openjdk-devel
  - name: Install Maven
    ansible.builtin.dnf:
      name: maven
```

That's one valid way, but with loops, you could rewrite the playbook to something more compact:

```
tasks:
  - name: Install Packages
    ansible.builtin.dnf:
      name: "{{ item }}" ❶
    loop: [ 'java-17-openjdk-devel', 'maven'] ❷
```

❶ Runs the `dnf` command against the value of the variable `item`

❷ Loops through the array of elements, setting the value in the `item` variables

Both playbooks are equivalent, but notice that the last one is more compact and maintainable; to add new packages, only add a new element to the list.

In this example, you set the list directly in the loop as constant, but a custom variable could be used and set in any of the ways explained in Chapter 4.

It's possible to use a list of hashes referencing subkeys in the `item` variable by adding a dot and appending the key name.

The following example copies files from the local directory to managed hosts:

```
- name: Add several users
  - name: copy files
      ansible.builtin.copy:
        src: "{{item.src}}"
        dest: "{{item.dest}}"
  loop:
    - { src: 'ngnix.conf', dest: '/etc/nginx/conf.d/localhost.conf' }
    - { src: 'hosts.conf', dest: '/etc/hosts' }
```

To loop over a dictionary, you need to transform the variable as a list of dictionaries instead of a dictionary by calling the `dict2items` filter:

```
- name: Add several users
  ansible.builtin.user:
    name: "{{ item.name }}"
    state: present
    groups: "{{ item.groups }}"
  loop: "{{ userinfo | dict2items }}" ❶
  vars:
    userinfo: ❷
      name: alex
      groups: root
```

❶ Transforms the `userinfo` dictionary into a list of dictionaries

❷ Defines the variable as a dictionary

In some cases, you might need to rename the `item` variable to not overwrite the value of the inner and outer loops continuously (e.g., when using nested loops). To rename the variable `item`, use the `loop_var` directive. The following example changes the variable from `item` to `my_item`:

```
  loop: [ 'java-17-openjdk-devel', 'maven']
  loop_control:
    loop_var: my_item ❶
```

❶ Renames the loop variable

Registering Variables

In Chapter 4, you've seen how to capture task output using the `register` keyword. As a reminder:

```
tasks:
  - name: Echo var
    ansible.builtin.command: /bin/echo "Hello World {{msg_name}}"
    register: response
  - name: Print result
    ansible.builtin.debug:
      var: response
```

But when looping, Ansible executes the task multiple times, so what's the value of the registered variable when the loop finishes?

When using loops, the *result* structure changes to accommodate the multiple results. The variable will contain a `results` section of the type array, with the first position of the array, the result of the first iteration, and so on.

Let's write a playbook that iterates through a list of elements, executes an echo command, and registers the result to print it in the console:

```
- name: Echoing in loops
  hosts: all
  tasks:
    - name: Echo var
      ansible.builtin.command: /bin/echo "Hello World {{item}}" ❶
      loop: [ 'Ada', 'Aixa'] ❷
      register: response  ❸
    - name: Print result
      debug:
        var: response
```

❶ echo task definition

❷ Loop with two elements

❸ Registers the output of each loop

Run the playbook with a proper inventory file to get the content of the `response` variable registered within a loop:

```
ansible-playbook -i inventory playbook-loop.yaml
```

And you'll get the following output:

```
ok: [192.168.1.115] => {
    "response": {
        "changed": true,
        "msg": "All items completed",
        "results": [
            { ❶
                "ansible_loop_var": "item",
                "changed": true,
                "cmd": [
                    "/bin/echo",
                    "Hello World Ada"
                ]
                ...
            },
            { ❷
                "ansible_loop_var": "item",
                "changed": true,
                "cmd": [
                    "/bin/echo",
                    "Hello World Aixa"
                ],
                ...
            }
        ],
```

```
        "skipped": false
    }
```

❶ Result of the first iteration

❷ Result of the second iteration

During the iteration, the result of the current item is placed in the registered variable.

Pausing

Sometimes you might need to pause the execution between each element in a loop. Use the `pause` directive in the `loop_control` section to set the number of seconds to wait until the following element is processed:

```
loop: [ 'Ada', 'Aixa']
loop_control:
  pause: 5 ❶
```

❶ Waits 5 seconds before processing the following item of the list.

Indexing

It's possible to track the current index of iteration using the `index_var` directive to specify the variable name to contain the current loop index:

```
tasks:
  - name: Echo var
    ansible.builtin.command: >-
      /bin/echo "Hello World from element number {{idx}}" ❶
    loop:
      - 'Ada'
      - 'Aixa'
    loop_control:
      index_var: idx ❷
```

❶ Prints the index of the current element in the remote node

❷ Defines `idx` as the tracking variable

Special Variables

Any list variable is susceptible to being iterated in a loop. In Ansible, there is a group of special variables that represents the list of hosts. Even though you can also use them in any situation, they fit perfectly in loops and conditionals to execute a task over a specific set of hosts. Some of these variables are:

`ansible_play_batch`
: A list of hostnames that are in scope for the current `batch` of the play.

`ansible_play_hosts`
: The list of all hosts still active in the current play.

`groups`
: A list of all the groups (and hosts) in the inventory; you can enumerate all hosts within a group using the array construction `groups['all']`.

The following playbook prints all hosts belonging to the `therock` group:

```
- name: Show therock the hosts in the inventory
  ansible.builtin.debug:
    msg: "{{ item }}"
  loop: "{{ groups['therock'] }}" ❶
```

❶ Returns the hosts of `therock` group.

Querying Inventory Hostnames

Besides using variables to select hosts, Ansible offers a specific lookup plug-in named `inventory_hostnames` that is used with `query` to get a list of hosts using *patterns*.

For example, to select all hosts except the ones under the `dbservers` group, you use `query` in a loop, like this:

```
- name: Show all hosts except db
  ansible.builtin.debug:
    msg: "{{ item }}"
  loop: "{{ query('inventory_hostnames', 'all:!dbservers') }}"
```

Apart from host variables, some variables are only available within a loop to get extended loop information, such as its first iteration, the last iteration, or the number of elements. To access these variables, set the `extended` directive to `true` in the `loop_control` section:

```
loop_control:
  extended: true
```

You can then use the following variables:

`ansible_loop.allitems`
: The list of all items in the loop.

`ansible_loop.index`
: The current iteration of the loop 1-based.

`ansible_loop.index0`
: The current iteration of the loop 0-based.

`ansible_loop.revindex`
: The number of iterations from the end of the loop 1-based.

`ansible_loop.revindex0`
: The number of iterations from the end of the loop 0-based.

`ansible_loop.first`
: True if first iteration.

`ansible_loop.last`
: True if last iteration.

`ansible_loop.length`
: The number of items in the loop.

`ansible_loop.previtem`
: The item from the previous iteration of the loop. Undefined during the first iteration.

`ansible_loop.nextitem`
: The item from the following iteration of the loop. Undefined during the last iteration.

So far, you've iterated over a task looping over a list of elements. In the following section, you'll learn how to iterate over a task until a condition is met.

Retrying Tasks Until a Condition Is Met

You can assume that if an Ansible task worked in the past, it will work every time if nothing has changed. That's true until there are external factors you don't control, such as network connectivity. For example, a task to install a package in the managed host succeeds now because the package manager is up and running, but in two days the task can fail because, at that time, the package manager server is down.

Usually, these errors are temporal glitches; after some seconds, everything works as expected. To automatically fix these errors, Ansible lets you retry a task until a condition is met.

The following snippet retries a task until the output of the task executed on the managed host contains the word `succeeded`. At most, 5 retries with a delay of 10 seconds between each attempt are executed:

```
- name: Retry a task until a certain condition is met
  ansible.builtin.command: ...
  register: result ❶
```

```
until: result.stdout.find("succeeded") != -1 ❷
retries: 5 ❸
delay: 10 ❹
```

❶ Output is registered.

❷ If the result of any attempt has succeeded in its stdout, the task is not retried.

❸ Task runs up to five times.

❹ A delay of 10 seconds between each attempt.

To see the results of individual retries, run the play with -vv.

This approach is valid in idempotent modules. In the case of nonidempotent modules, a retry might leave the system in an unstable state. Check the module documentation to know if it is idempotent or not, and which side effects might cause the re-execution of the module.

In this section, you've learned how to execute a task multiple times. In the following section, you'll see how to control whether Ansible executes a task.

Conditionals

Ansible provides conditionals to evaluate whether a task, role, or import should be executed.

Suppose you need to install a new package. For example, if you are managing multiple hosts with different operating systems, Fedora and Debian, you might need two different tasks, one to execute `dnf` and another to execute `apt-get`. The first task is executed only in hosts with Fedora installed, while the second task is executed only in hosts with Debian installed. How do you filter the execution of a task by the operative system?

Ansible offers the `when` directive to evaluate the task execution. It supports all Jinja2 standard tests and filters in conditionals. Conditional expressions can contain Ansible facts, registered variables, or Ansible variables to compare with other values.

First Example with a Conditional

Let's take the problem introduced at the beginning of this section and write a playbook that installs a package using the correct package manager:

```
- name: Install ngnix
  hosts: all
  become: true ❶
  tasks:
  - name: install nginx in Fedora
    ansible.builtin.dnf::
      name: nginx
    when: ansible_facts['distribution'] == "Fedora" ❷
  - name: install nginx in Debian
    ansible.builtin.apt:
      name: ngnix
    when: ansible_facts['distribution'] == "Debian"
```

❶ Becomes root to install the package

❷ Gets an Ansible fact and compares it with a string

Execute the following command to run the playbook:

```
ansible-playbook -i inventory -K playbook-facts.yaml
```

The running of the playbook shows the execution of the Fedora task:

```
...
TASK [Gathering Facts]
ok: [192.168.1.115]

TASK [install nginx in Fedora]
ok: [192.168.1.115] ❶

TASK [install nginx in Debian]
skipping: [192.168.1.115] ❷
...
```

❶ Runs the task in Fedora

❷ Skips Debian

You can store Ansible facts as variables to use for conditional logic. This is useful for creating readable playbooks, especially when a lot of facts are used. Let's rewrite the previous example, setting a fact as a variable:

```
- name: Install ngnix
  hosts: all
  become: true
  tasks:
  - name: Get the distribution
    ansible.builtin.set_fact: ❶
      distribution: "{{ ansible_facts['distribution'] }}" ❷
  - name: install nginx in Fedora
    ansible.builtin.dnf:
      name: nginx
```

```
    when: distribution == "Fedora"
  - name: install nginx in Debian
    ansible.builtin.apt:
      name: ngnix
    when: distribution == "Debian"
```

❶ Sets facts as variables

❷ Gets the distribution fact and sets it as var

Conditionals are very intuitive, and you can use them in multiple situations. In the next section, you'll explore some examples.

Using Conditionals

So far, you've seen conditionals with Ansible facts. Let's learn how to use conditionals with registered variables. Then, we'll show you how to use conditionals with standard variables.

Conditionals with registered variables

Often, in a playbook, you want to execute or skip a task based on the outcome of an earlier task. For example, you may want to check if a configuration file exists, and if not, copy it, or depending on the content of a file, execute a task or not.

The following playbook verifies if a file is present and if not, copies it from the local directory:

```
- name: Check file
  hosts: all
  tasks:
  - name: Check if file already exists
    ansible.builtin.command: ls /home/alex/application.properties
    register: file_exists
    ignore_errors: yes ❶
  - name: Copy conf file for the app
    ansible.builtin.copy:
      src: application.properties
      dest: /home/alex/application.properties
    when: file_exists is failed ❷
```

❶ Ansible interrupts a play if the command fails. With this option, Ansible continues executing the rest of the tasks.

❷ If the previous task fails, it executes this one.

Executing the playbook, you get the following output:

```
TASK [Gathering Facts]
ok: [192.168.1.115]
```

```
TASK [Check if file already exists]
fatal: [192.168.1.115]: FAILED! => {"changed": true, "cmd": ["ls", "/home/alex/
application.properties"], "delta": "0:00:00.011441", "end": "2024-01-25
13:39:25.941884", "msg": "non-zero return code", "rc": 2, ...
...ignoring ❶

TASK [Copy conf file for the app]
changed: [192.168.1.115] ❷
```

❶ The task fails because the file doesn't exist.

❷ The playbook is not terminated, and the file is copied.

Apart from registered variables, you can use standard variables in conditionals, too.

Conditionals with standard variables

As with registered variables, you can also use variables you define in the playbooks with conditionals. In the following example, Ansible executes a task depending on the Boolean value set in a variable:

```
- name: Check file
  hosts: all
  vars:
    special: false
  tasks:
  - name: Run the command if not special
    ansible.builtin.shell: echo "Not special"
    when: not special
```

The task is executed by default as the variable value matches the conditional expression. You can skip the execution of the task by setting the `special` variable to `true`, for example, overriding from the command line with the `--extra-vars` option:

```
ansible-playbook -i inventory --extra-vars="special=true" playbook-var.yaml
```

So far, you've used conditions to control task execution, but you can use them in imports, includes, or rules.

Conditionals with Reusable Tasks

You can use conditionals with reusable task files, playbooks, or roles.

Conditions in imports

When you add a conditional to an import statement, Ansible applies the condition to all tasks defined in the imported file.

For example, to import a playbook only if the host_type variable is set to db, you can write the following playbook:

```
- hosts: all
  tasks:
    - ansible.builtin.import_tasks: db_tasks.yaml
      when: host_type == 'db'
```

Notice that all tasks defined in the *db_tasks.yaml* file will implicitly have the when: host_type == 'db' condition.

Conditions in includes

When you add a conditional to an include statement, the condition is applied only to the include task itself and not to any other tasks, in contrast to what you've seen with import.

The same example rewritten with include looks like this:

```
- hosts: all
  tasks:
    - ansible.builtin.include_tasks: db_tasks.yaml
      when: host_type == 'db'
```

Conditions in roles

You've not seen roles in depth yet, but this is an introduction. In Chapter 8, you'll learn more about roles, but for now, remember that you can add conditionals to decide whether to apply for a role or not.

For example, applying a role only when the host type is db:

```
- hosts: all
  roles:
     - role: geerlingguy.mysql ❶
       when: host_type == 'db'
```

❶ The fully qualified name of the role

Jinja2

As mentioned at the beginning of this section, Ansible uses Jinja2 expressions in conditionals. Let's explore some of the most used operators when using conditionals.

Here are the conditionals for comparing elements:

`==`
: Compares two objects for equality.

`!=`
: Compares two objects for inequality.

`>`
: True if the lefthand side is greater than the righthand side.

`>=`
: True if the lefthand side is greater than or equal to the righthand side.

`<`
: True if the lefthand side is less than the righthand side.

`<=`
: True if the lefthand side is less than or equal to the righthand side.

Let's look at some examples:

```
name == 'Natale'
age >=18
country != 'Unknown'
```

Here are the logic operators:

`and`
: Returns true if the left and the right operand are true.

`or`
: Returns true if the left or the right operand is true.

`not`
: Negates a statement (see below).

`(expr)`
: Parentheses group an expression.

Here are some examples of logic operators in action:

```
name == 'Elder' and age >=18
```

Here are the special operators for conditional expressions:

`in`
: Performs a sequence/mapping containment test.

`is`
: Performs a test.

`|`
: Applies a filter.

Let's look at some examples:

```
num_hosts in [1, 2, 3]

x is defined
```

```
test_list = ['192.24.2.1', 'host.fqdn', '192.168.32.0/24', ...]
test_list | ansible.netcommon.ipaddr ❶
```

❶ Only shows IP addresses (192.24.2.1, 192.168.32.0/24)

In the next section, we'll cover the concept of handlers and why they are important in the Ansible ecosystem.

Handlers

So far, tasks are always executed in the defined order. You can skip executing tasks by using conditionals. But there are also special tasks that are executed only if triggered by another task *at the end of a play*. These special tasks are *handlers* and typically are used to start, reload, restart, and stop services, among many other use cases you might need. For example, you may need to restart a service if a task updates the configuration of the service but not if nothing changes.

The `handlers` section in the YAML document sets the tasks that should be executed if triggered. The `notify` directive is used to trigger the handlers.

Let's create a simple playbook for updating a web page hosted in nginx, then restarting the service:

```
- name: Update page
  hosts: all
  become: true
  tasks:
    - name: copy index.html
      ansible.builtin.copy:
        src: index.html
        dest: /usr/share/nginx/html/index.html
        mode: 0644
      notify: ❶
        - Restart nginx ❷
    - ansible.builtin.debug:
        msg: 'Page updated'
  handlers: ❸
    - name: Restart nginx ❹
      ansible.builtin.service: ❺
        name: nginx
        state: restarted
```

❶ Notify a handler in case the task succeeds.

❷ Name of the handler to invoke.

❸ Registration of handlers.

❹ Registration of a handler with a name.

❺ The task to execute.

Run the playbook with the following command:

```
ansible-playbook -i inventory -K playbook-handler.yaml
BECOME password:

PLAY [Update page]
...

TASK [copy index.html]
changed: [192.168.1.115] ❶

TASK [ansible.builtin.debug]
ok: [192.168.1.115] => {
    "msg": "Page updated"
}

RUNNING HANDLER [Restart nginx] ❷ ❸
changed: [192.168.1.115]
```

❶ Copies the file and notifies the handler.

❷ Handlers are executed after all tasks.

❸ The copy task changed the host, invoking the handler.

It's important to note that if the task triggering the handler doesn't change the host, there is no invocation of the handler.

You can specify a list of handlers in the `notify` directive so all of them are notified in case of a change.

Handlers are executed in the order defined in the `handlers` section, not in the order listed in the `notify` statement. This is important to be aware of, especially if handlers need to be executed in order.

Our advice is not to have interdependencies between handlers.

Notifying the same handler multiple times will result in executing it only once, regardless of how many tasks notify it.

Grouping Handlers

As you've seen, you named the handlers, and you refer to them by their name. This is a good strategy when there aren't many handlers, but when you have a large list of handlers, and some of them are notified together, it's a good idea to keep them together in a group.

To create a group, use the `listen` directive when registering a handler. All handlers having the same name in the `listen` section belong to the same group and can be triggered together.

Let's see a simple example of notifying multiple handlers without and with using `listen`.

This first example doesn't use the `listen` directive:

```
tasks:
  - name: copy index.html
    ansible.builtin.copy:
      src: index.html
      dest: /usr/share/nginx/html/index.html
      mode: 0644
    notify: ❶
      - Restart nginx
      - Restart Infinispan
handlers:
  - name: Restart nginx
    ansible.builtin.service:
      name: nginx
      state: restarted
  - name: Restart Infinispan
    ansible.builtin.service:
      name: infinispan
      state: restarted
```

❶ Two handlers are triggered

In this second example, we create a group named `restart web services` using the `listen` directive:

```
tasks:
  - name: copy index.html
    ansible.builtin.copy:
      src: index.html
      dest: /usr/share/nginx/html/index.html
      mode: 0644
    notify: "restart web services" ❶
handlers:
  - name: Restart nginx
    ansible.builtin.service:
      name: nginx
```

```
        state: restarted
      listen: "restart web services" ❷
    - name: Restart Infinispan
      ansible.builtin.service:
        name: infinispan
        state: restarted
      listen: "restart web services" ❸
```

❶ Task notifies the group.

❷ This handler listens for the `restart web services` trigger.

❸ This handler is executed together with the previous one.

When multiple handlers are triggered together, it's a good idea to use `listen` to keep them grouped.

Flushing Handlers

Ansible executes handlers after task execution. This approach is perfect because the handler only runs once, regardless of how many tasks notify it.

But in some situations, you might want to flush handlers in the middle of a play.

Ansible has *meta tasks*—special tasks that can influence Ansible's internal execution or state. One of these meta tasks is `flush_handlers`, which executes all triggered handler tasks. Moreover, it empties the queue of handlers to be executed; hence, if any other task triggers an already executed handler, it will be executed again.

To execute a meta task, use the `meta` directive:

```
tasks:
  - name: Copy index.html
    ansible.builtin.copy: ...

  - name: Flush handlers
    ansible.builtin.meta: flush_handlers ❶

  - name: Copy configuration
    ansible.builtin.copy: ... ❷
```

❶ All of the handlers triggered in previous tasks are executed.

❷ All of the handlers triggered after the flush are executed.

Avoid using variables in the handler name. If a variable is not available, the entire play fails.

So far, we've seen how to control the flow of Ansible in typical cases. In the next section, you'll see how to handle error situations.

Error Management

So far, we've run Ansible in a controlled way, with no failures and tasks completed correctly, but this is not always the case. Tasks might fail because the executed command fails, the managed host is unavailable, or the playbook definition contains a runtime error (i.e., variable not set).

In these cases, Ansible stops executing on that host and continues on other hosts. But this behavior might not fit in all situations; sometimes, a command failure is the expected result, or a failure in a host should stop executions to all hosts.

Ignoring Failed Commands

When a command fails, Ansible stops the execution of further tasks on the failing host. Using the `ignore_errors` directive in a task will make Ansible continue executing tasks despite the error.

Remember that the ignore errors directive only affects when the task returns a failure. With Ansible, errors like undefined variables, connection issues, and so on will stop tasks regardless of the value of `ignore_errors`.

```
- name: Try to show content of not existing file
  ansible.builtin.command: cat /etc/a.txt
  ignore_errors: true
- name: Show the content of an existing file
  ansible.builtin.command: cat /etc/b.txt ❶
  ignore_errors: true
```

❶ Even though the first command fails, the second command runs too.

If you want to ignore the unreachable hosts error, use `ignore_unreachable` at the task or playbook level.

About Handlers

As explained in the previous section, handlers are executed at the end of each play. If there is any failure in any tasks for a specific host, handlers will not run for that host. For example, task 1 runs on host 1, succeeds, and notifies handler 1. Then task 2 runs on host 1 and fails. Handler 1 will never be executed on host 1 even though it was triggered on a successful task.

To change the default behavior, use the `--force-handlers` CLI option, set `force_handlers: true` in the play, or configure Ansible with `force_handlers = true` to make failing hosts also receive notifications.

Defining Failure

From the point of view of Ansible, a task fails when the command it executes fails and finishes with an error code.

Sometimes a command might notify the failure through a console message instead of returning an error code (an integer with a value greater than 0). Or the failure is based on a business logic output instead of a command failure. For example, a task should fail if the background color of a web page is red; in this specific case, the `curl` command succeeds as the web page is up and running, but the task should fail as the content is not.

The `failed_when` directive lets you define when a task should fail based on a registered variable containing the command result. Usually, a variable with a command result contains:

- The exit code (`rc` field)
- If the host changed (`changed` field)
- The standard error output (`stderr` field)
- The executed command (`cmd` field)
- The standard output (`stdout` field)
- Many more ...

Let's code a playbook failing when the web page body content contains the word *bye*. To fetch the page, you'll use the `uri` module, used to interact with HTTP and HTTPS web pages:

```
- name: Checks Site
  hosts: all
  tasks:
    - name: Fetch webpage
      ansible.builtin.uri: ❶
        url: http://mysite.com
        return_content: true
```

```
        register: output ❷
        failed_when: "'bye' in output.content" ❸
```

❶ Uses the uri module to fetch web content

❷ Registers response in output var

❸ Sets to fail the task if the result is an error or the page content contains the word *bye*

You can use any conditional expression in the failed_when directive, for example:

```
failed_when: output.rc == 0 or output.changed == true

failed_when: ❶
  - result.rc > 0
  - "'No such' not in result.stdout"
```

❶ By default, Ansible uses the and operator when not otherwise specified.

Defining Change

When a playbook finishes its execution, Ansible provides a report with statistics like executed tasks and failed tasks. You can see the previous execution report in the following snippet:

```
PLAY RECAP 192.168.1.115  : ok=2  changed=0  unreachable=0  failed=0
skipped=0  rescued=0  ignored=0
```

What we are focusing on in this section is the changed report. When an action (module/task) changes something, like installing a package on the managed host, it reports a changed status to Ansible. On the other hand, if there are no changes, and it is left to the module to decide if there are changes or not, then it reports an ok status.

But consider our previous example. Since the URL request returns a 200 status code, Ansible registers the task as an ok, but what if you know that calling this service, even though it returns a 200 status code, has changed the host? Ansible lets you define when a particular task has changed a remote host using the changed_when conditional. Redefine the previous example to report the call as changed instead of ok:

```
- name: Checks Site
  hosts: all
  tasks:
    - name: Fetch webpage
      ansible.builtin.uri:
        url: http://mysite.com
        return_content: true
```

```
    register: output
    changed_when: "output.status == 200" ❶
```

❶ Changes when the status code is 200

The report will show one task as changed.

Aborting a Play

When a task fails on a single host, all functions of other hosts continue their execution. But sometimes, you might want to ensure that all tasks are successful in all hosts, and if there is any problem in any of them, you want to stop the execution and not continue on other hosts.

In such cases, when setting `any_errors_fatal` to `true` and the task returns an error, Ansible finishes the errored task on all hosts in the current batch and stops executing the play on all hosts.

One of the use cases of this flag is creating a barrier between the execution of groups of hosts. For example, you could create a task executed against some hosts. Only if the execution of the task succeeds for all hosts can the execution continue with the rest of the tasks and hosts.

Let's see this in a playbook:

```
- hosts: frontends
  any_errors_fatal: true ❶

  tasks:
    - name: Publish under maintenance page ❷
      ansible.builtin.copy: ....

- hosts: backends ❸

  tasks:
    - name: Stop service
      ansible.builtin.service: ....

    - name: Update backend
      ansible.builtin.copy: ....

    - name: Start Service
      ansible.builtin.service: ....
```

❶ If any task fails in the `frontends` host, the playbook execution is aborted.

❷ Copies the maintenance page to `frontends` hosts.

❸ If all `frontends` hosts have the maintenance page, then the update of the `backends` host is executed.

By default, Ansible will execute backend tasks even though a failure in frontend tasks is thrown. In this example, we used the `any_error_fatal: true` directive on frontend hosts to abort the process if there is an error. So the process of rolling updates cannot start until the frontend has been updated with the maintenance page.

You can also abort the play when a certain threshold of failures has been reached using the `max_fail_percentage` directive. For example, setting `max_fail_percentage: 50` will make Ansible stop execution if 50% of the tasks fail.

Blocks

Ansible playbooks can contain as many tasks as required for maintaining your infrastructure. However, maintaining playbooks with a huge amount of tasks might be challenging.

One of the options Ansible offers is grouping tasks in *blocks*. Blocks create logical groups of tasks where all tasks inherit directives set at the block level. Any directive set at the block level does not affect the block itself; it is only inherited by the tasks enclosed by a block.

Blocks also offer a way to handle task errors at the block level and fix these errors in a single place.

To define a block, wrap the list of tasks belonging to a block under the `block` directive. All directives at the same level of `block` are inherited for all tasks defined within the block. For example, setting the `become_user` directive at the block level makes all tasks enclosed in the block run as the user set there.

Grouping Tasks with Blocks

Let's create a block containing two simple tasks to update a web page deployed in ngnix. The first task copies the page into the ngnix shared directory, and the second restarts the ngnix service.

Moreover, the playbook contains a condition affecting the block execution. Only when the `update_page` variable is set to `true` will the tasks within the block be executed:

```
- name: Web Servers tasks
  hosts: webservers
  tasks:
   - name: Update pages
     block: ❶
        - name: copy index.html
```

```
        ansible.builtin.copy:
          src: index.html
          dest: /usr/share/nginx/html/index.html
          mode: 0644

      - name: restart nginx
        ansible.builtin.service:
          name: nginx
          state: restarted
    when: update_page == true ❷
```

❶ Block defining two tasks.

❷ Condition is evaluated before Ansible executes tasks in the block.

Let's explore how to handle errors with blocks.

Error Handling with Blocks

You've already seen how to handle error situations in Ansible in the previous section. Using blocks, you can control how Ansible responds to task errors by providing custom execution in case of errors.

Let's abstract from Ansible (and YAML) to talk about how programming languages handle errors, and let's pick Java. Error handling syntax in Java uses the `try/catch/finally` form:

```
try { ❶
    insertIntoDb();
} catch (Exception e) {
    exceptionLogic(); ❷
} finally {
    closeConnection(); ❸
}
```

❶ Executes business logic

❷ In case of an error, executes this logic

❸ Always executes this code after a try or after the catch

Ansible blocks let you reproduce similar construction but execute tasks instead of code. Two directives are used: `rescue`, equivalent to the `catch` clause in Java, and `always`, equivalent to the `finally` clause.

The following snippet shows the structure of an Ansible block with error handling:

```
tasks:
  - name: Update pages
    block:
```

```
    - name: Task 1
      ...
    - name: Task 2
      ...
  rescue:
    - name: Exception logic
      ...
  always:
    - name: Executes after all
      ...
```

rescue and always are optional and can be used alone or together.

Let's create a straightforward playbook that installs an invalid package, catches the error, and finally executes some logic:

```
- name: Block example
  hosts: all
  tasks:
  - name: Attempt to install a package
    block:
      - name: install an invalid package
        ansible.builtin.dnf:
          name: qwehdjikn
    rescue:
      - ansible.builtin.debug:
          msg: 'Oh there is an error'
    always:
      - ansible.builtin.debug:
          msg: 'This always executes'
```

If you run this playbook, you get the following output:

```
ASK [install an invalid package] ❶
fatal: [192.168.1.115]: FAILED! => {"changed": false, "msg": "This command has
to be run under the root user.", "results": []}

TASK [ansible.builtin.debug] ❷
ok: [192.168.1.115] => {
    "msg": "Oh there is an error"
}

TASK [ansible.builtin.debug] ❸
ok: [192.168.1.115] => {
    "msg": "This always executes"
}
```

❶ Executes a failing task.

❷ The `rescue` task catches the error.

❸ Task executed at the end of the block.

Blocks offer a convenient way of dealing with errors in a similar way as programming languages do.

Conclusion

In this chapter, you've learned about flow control, executing a task multiple times, changing the input parameters, and the concept of blocks. The next chapter will cover how to manage files and resources, with a focus on templating.

CHAPTER 6

Managing Files and Resources

Managing hosts is much more than just installing and updating software, creating users, or restarting a service. It also involves copying applications or configuration files to managed hosts.

This chapter covers different modules to manipulate files in Ansible, ranging from copying files from the control node to the managed node, to creating templates. Speaking about templates, you'll get an introduction to the Jinja2 template engine as it's used in Ansible to render manifests.

Modules to Manage Files and Folders

In this section, we'll explore several modules that can be used to manipulate files in Ansible.

file Module

The `file` module has the following purposes:

- It sets attributes (ownership, group, permissions) for files, directories, and symbolic links.
- It deletes remote content like files, directories, or symbolic links.

To change the ownership, group, and permission of a file, run:

```
- name: Change file ownership, group, and permissions
  ansible.builtin.file:
    path: /home/alex/application.properties
    owner: natale
    group: devs
    mode: '0644' ❶
```

❶ Quote for octal number parsing

To create a symbolic link, use the `src` field as the path the symbolic link will refer to, the `dest` as the path where the symbolic link is placed, and the `state` field as `link`:

```
- name: Create a symbolic link
  ansible.builtin.file:
    src: /proc/meminfo ❶
    dest: /home/alex/meminfo ❷
    owner: alex
    group: alex
    state: link ❸
```

❶ Path of the file to link to

❷ Destination link

❸ Set to `hard` to create a hard symbolic link

To create a directory, use the `path` field to set the directory location and the `state` field to `directory`:

```
- name: Create a directory if it does not exist
  ansible.builtin.file:
    path: /etc/some_directory
    state: directory
    mode: '0755'
```

The file module can be used to change not only the owner, group, or permissions, but also other file attributes, such as access or modification time:

```
- name: Update modification and access time ❶
  ansible.builtin.file:
    path: /etc/some_file
    state: file
    modification_time: now
    access_time: now
```

❶ If user/group are not specified, the Ansible login user is used to manage the node.

One important parameter is `recursive`. When it's set to `true`, Ansible applies the change recursively on the directory contents. This parameter is only valid when `state` is `directory`:

```
- name: Recursively change ownership of a directory
  ansible.builtin.file:
    path: /home/alex
    state: directory
    recurse: yes
```

```
    owner: alex
    group: alex
```

archive/unarchive Module

The `archive` module creates a compressed archive of one or more files on the managed host. It doesn't copy any content from the control to the managed host or vice versa; it only compresses the content. To move the content, use the `copy` module instead.

On the other hand, the `unarchive` module does the opposite: it decompresses a file located on the managed host.

Let's explore some examples using both the `archive` and `unarchive` module. First, let's create a backup of the web page deployed in nginx by compressing the contents into a *zip* archive:

```
- name: Compress directory
  ansible.builtin.archive:
    path: /usr/share/nginx/html ❶
    dest: /opt/website-backup.zip ❷
    format: zip ❸
    owner: root
    group: root
```

❶ Directory to compress

❷ Ouput file

❸ Compression format

Supported formats include: `bz2`, `gz`, `tar`, `xz`, and `zip`.

The `path` parameter supports setting a list of multiple files or a globbed path to select the entries to compress. Moreover, the `exclude_path` parameter lets you exclude specific directories or files from being archived. For example, the following task creates a *.gz* file with the web page content but not including files and folders beginning with `logs`:

```
- name: Create a backup without logs
  ansible.builtin.archive:
    path:
    - /usr/share/nginx/html/*
    dest: /opt/website-backup.gz
    exclude_path:
    - /usr/share/nginx/html/logs*
    format: gz
```

To decompress a file, use the `unarchive` module. This module copies and decompresses the archive from the control node to the managed/remote host.

If the backup file created previously is located on the control node, you can decompress the contents into the nginx content directory by running the following task:

```
- name: Extract webpage
  ansible.builtin.unarchive:
    src: website-backup.gz ❶
    dest: /usr/share/nginx/html/ ❷
```

❶ Local file

❷ Remote directory to decompress the contents

The previous task copies the *website-backup.gz* file from the local machine to the remote host and decompresses it within the */usr/share/nginx/html/* directory.

If the compressed file is already on the remote host, Ansible can decompress the file if you set the `remote_src` parameter to `true`:

```
- name: Unarchive a file that is already on the remote machine
  ansible.builtin.unarchive:
    src: /opt/website-backup.gz
    dest: /usr/share/nginx/html/
    remote_src: true ❶
```

❶ Specify that the file is already on the remote host.

assemble Module

In some situations, you might need to build up a configuration file from multiple sources. The *conf.d* directory is a common option in many applications that is used to to merge multiple configuration files. Ansible provides the `assemble` module to take a directory of files (local or already placed in the managed host) and concatenates them to produce a new file in the specified destination. Multiple configuration files are read in alphabetic order.

The following task assembles local files and copies the result to the managed host:

```
- name: Assemble from fragments from a directory
  ansible.builtin.assemble:
    src: /tmp/app/fragments
    dest: /etc/app/application.properties
    owner: root
    group: root
    mode: '644'
    regexp: 'conf$' ❶
```

❶ Only joins files ending with `conf`

When fragments are already placed on the managed host, set `remote_src` to `true` to avoid Ansible searching for fragments on the local machine.

copy Module

You have been using the `copy` module in the previous chapters, but it's good to review its functionality in detail as it is an important module to utilize when managing files; it's used to copy files from the local/control node to the remote node. You can use the `copy` module to copy files between directories in the remote host or generate a file on the remote host with the given content.

To copy files between remote host directories, use the `remote_src` parameter:

```
- name: Copy a file on the remote machine
  ansible.builtin.copy:
    src: /etc/hosts
    dest: /etc/hosts.edit
    remote_src: yes
    owner: root
    group: root
    mode: u+rw,g-wx,o-rwx ❶
```

❶ Mode set in symbolic fashion

Another option is to create inline content of the file inside the playbook and copy the resulting file to the remote host:

```
- name: Copy using inline content
  ansible.builtin.copy:
    content: 'connection_pool=true'
    dest: /etc/app/application.properties.fragment1
    backup: true ❶
```

❶ If the same file exists, create a backup file, including the timestamp information.

However, the `copy` module does not cover the use case of copying a file from a remote node to the control node.

fetch Module

The `fetch` module performs the opposite operation by copying assets from the remote node to the control node:

```
- name: Store file into /tmp/fetched/host.example.com/etc/hosts
  ansible.builtin.fetch:
    src: /etc/hosts ❶
    dest: /tmp ❷
```

❶ The file to retrieve on the remote system. The contents must be a file.

❷ A directory to save the file into.

Since `fetch` might be executed against multiple hosts, Ansible creates a directory structure with information about the hostname. Files fetched from remote hosts are not overridden as they are copied to the local directory.

The layout is the `dest` directory, then as subfolders `<hostname>/<src>`, and finally the filename. So the directory layout for the previous `copy` command, assuming the hostname was `db.example.com`, would be:

```
.
├── tmp ❶
│   └── db.example.com
│       └── etc ❷
│           └── hosts ❸
```

❶ `dest` directory

❷ Hostname + `src` directory

❸ Filename

stat Module

In Chapter 5, you read about conditionals. You may often need to apply conditionals, depending on the status of a directory or file. For example, you may need to execute a task if the target is a symbolic link or if it is a directory. Also, you might need to retrieve the resource's ownership, group, and permissions.

The `stat` module retrieves facts for a file or directory. This code will execute a debug task only if a given file is a directory:

```
- ansible.builtin.stat:
    path: /home/alex
  register: sym
- ansible.builtin.debug:
    msg: "Path exists and is a directory."
  when: sym.stat.isdir is defined and sym.stat.isdir
```

line/block infile Module

When managing hosts, you commonly need to insert, delete, or update a line from a configuration file (i.e., updating the *hosts* file). The `lineinfile` module adds, modifies, removes, or replaces a line or multiple lines in the managed host's configuration files.

Let's start with the simplest example of adding and removing a line from a file:

```
- name: Insert line
  ansible.builtin.lineinfile:
    line: Hello Alexandra ❶
    path: /home/alex/welcome.txt ❷
    create: true ❸
- name: Remove line
  ansible.builtin.lineinfile:
    line: Hello World ❹
    path: /home/alex/welcome.txt
    state: absent ❺
```

❶ Line to add.

❷ File to add the line to.

❸ Create the file if it does not exist.

❹ Line to remove.

❺ Specify that the line should be removed.

In the previous example, the line was added at the end of the file since no conditions were present that specified an alternate location. However, some files require you to modify a line in a specific place. A typical use case is within *ini* files. To specify the location where lines should be appended, use the `insertafter` parameter. For example, given the following *ini* file:

```
[database]
server = localhost

[memcache]
buffersize = 23
```

If you want to add a port for the database, it must occur within the `database` section instead of at the end of the file. Let's create a task adding the port in the correct location after the `server` definition:

```
- name: Set the port value in the database category
  ansible.builtin.lineinfile:
    insertafter: server
    line: port = 5432
    path: /home/alex/conf.ini
```

Use the `insertbefore` property to insert before the desired line within the file.

The examples thus far are the simplest for the `lineinfile` module. Moving forward, imagine that you have the following configuration file:

```
# many more properties here
connectionpool=50
threadpool=25
# and many more properties here
```

To update both properties with different values, use the `lineinfile` module together with a `loop`:

```
- name: Change configuration properties
  ansible.builtin.lineinfile:
    regexp: "{{ item.regexp }}" ❶
    line: "{{ item.line }}" ❷
    path: /home/alex/application.properties
  loop: ❸
    - line: "connectionpool=100"
      regexp: ^connectionpool
    - line: "threadpool=250"
      regexp: ^threadpool
```

❶ Sets a regular expression to search for in the file

❷ New line value

❸ Loop section with the specified parameter values

When Ansible executes this task, the *application.properties* file is updated with the new values.

To check if a specific line is present in a file, you can use the `check_mode` attribute of the task:

```
- name: Check for line
  ansible.builtin.lineinfile:
    line: Hello Alexandra
    path: /home/alex/welcome.txt
  check_mode: true ❶
  register: line_check

- name: Print message
  ansible.builtin.debug:
    msg: Not Hello Alexandra.
    when: line_check.changed ❷
```

❶ `check_mode` parameter checks if the task changes the file.

❷ Validates if the file changed or not.

So far, you've used the `lineinfile` module to manipulate a single line. But what happens if you want to add several lines of text instead of a single line? The `blockinfile` module manipulates multiline text surrounded by customizable marker lines.

To append multiline text in a file, use the following task:

```
- name: Insert multiline content
  ansible.builtin.blockinfile:
    path: /home/alex/welcome.txt
    create: true
    block: | ❶
      Hello Ada
      Hello World
```

❶ Defines the content to add to the file. The | specifies a multiline content.

Sometimes you need to place content in a specific location instead of at the end of the file. The `insertafter`/`insertbefore` parameters can be used in this case.

This `blockinfile` module adds a marker between the defined text. You can customize the message that is used with the `marker` parameter. The default value is `# BEGIN/END ANSIBLE MANAGED BLOCK`.

Common Configuration Parameters for Modules

Most of the modules that manipulate files have common parameters, such as `owner`, `group`, or `mode`. However, there are other additional parameters that can be specified, as summarized in Table 6-1.

Table 6-1. Common parameters

Parameter	Description
`attributes`	The attributes of the resulting filesystem. To get supported flags, check the man page for `chattr` on the target system.
`backup`	Create a backup file, including the timestamp information.
`create`	Create a new file if it does not exist.
`selevel`	The level part of the SELinux filesystem object context.
`serole`	The role part of the SELinux filesystem object context.
`setype`	The type part of the SELinux filesystem object context.
`seuser`	The user part of the SELinux filesystem object context.
`unsafe_writes`	Influence when to use atomic operation to prevent data corruption or inconsistent reads from the target filesystem object.
`validate`	The validation command to run before copying the updated file to the final destination.

In the first part of this chapter, you learned how to manipulate files or change them using `block/lineinfile` modules.

Although this approach works, and it is the convenient way when the configuration file is not a part of the application (i.e., */etc/hosts* or */etc/sudoers* or */etc/ssh/sshd_config*), it is not the most optimal for application configuration files.

In the following section, you will learn about templates that you can use to create a skeleton of a configuration file (or any other file) and fill the placeholders at runtime.

Templates

Deploying an application to multiple environments with Ansible is easy because the same playbook is run against different groups of hosts defined in the inventory. The challenge with configuration files is that the properties of one environment may differ from those in another environment. For example, the connection pool of a datasource may be lower in a preproduction environment than in production.

One way to resolve this problem is to have multiple configuration files (i.e., *application.properties.pre*, *application.properties.prod*, etc.), copy them to the managed host, and rename them to the desired filename. However, this approach has several drawbacks:

- You can copy the wrong configuration file to the wrong environment.
- Changing a parameter name requires changing multiple files.
- There are additional files to maintain.

To avoid these challenges, Ansible supports the Jinja2 templating language for creating template files, rendering them at runtime, and copying the rendered files to the managed host, replacing the placeholders with Ansible facts, variables, or custom variables. With templates, updating configuration files becomes easier; you only have to perform the changes in one location, and all environments will receive the change.

Let's create a template file for an application with the following configurations:

- The creation date and time of the configuration file
- The current hostname
- The connection pool value depends on the amount of memory available in the host
- The username and password to connect to a database

The first three parameters are set using variables provided by Ansible, and the last one is set using any of the methods introduced previously.

By default, templates are stored in the *templates* directory, so Ansible reads them automatically without needing to specify them explicitly. Create the *templates* directory, and create a file called *conf.properties.j2* with the following content:

```
# File created at {{ansible_date_time.iso8601}} ❶

hostname={{ ansible_hostname }}


{% if ansible_memtotal_mb > 500 %} ❷
connection_pool=30
{% else %}
connection_pool=10
{% endif %}


db_username={{ username }} ❸
db_password={{ password }}
```

❶ Ansible variable to get the current date and time of the node when the facts were gathered

❷ Jinja2 conditional statement

❸ Custom variables

To render this template into a file, use the `template` module.

Create a new playbook file called *playbook.yaml* in the root directory, making use of the template module and setting the custom variable values in the `vars` section:

```
---
- name: configuration template
  hosts: all
  vars: ❶
    - username: Alex
    - password: Alex
  tasks:
    - name: Copy conf files
      ansible.builtin.template: ❷
        src: "conf.properties.j2" ❸
        dest: "/tmp/conf.properties" ❹
    - name: Display conf.properties contents
      ansible.builtin.command: cat conf.properties chdir=/tmp
      register: command_output
    - name: Print to console ❺
      ansible.builtin.debug:
        msg: "{{command_output.stdout.split('\n')}}"
```

❶ Definition of variables

❷ Template module

❸ Location of the template within the *templates* directory

❹ Remote destination directory

❺ Prints the resulting file

The output of the debug task would be similar to the following:

```
ok: [192.168.1.115] => {
    "msg": [
        "# File created at 2024-02-21T13:13:28Z",
        "",
        "hostname=localhost",
        "",
        "",
        "connection_pool=30",
        "",
        "",
        "db_username=Alex ",
        "db_password=Alex"
    ]
}
```

For simplicity, you set the sensitive data (username and password) directly in the playbook. However, in the real-world example, you would use a tool like Ansible Vault or integrate with a secrets management engine.

As with any other module involved in file management, attributes like `owner`, `mode`, `backup`, etc., are also supported.

You can also use templating in playbooks directly by templating task names and more. All templating occurs on the Ansible control node before the task is sent and executed on the target machine.

Jinja2

Ansible uses Jinja2 templating (*https://oreil.ly/iZFq2*) to enable dynamic expressions for accessing variables and facts. You can use all of the standard filters and tests included in Jinja2, additional specialized filters for selecting and transforming data, and tests for evaluating template expressions. Moreover, Ansible includes lookup plug-ins that can be used to retrieve data from external sources, such as files, APIs, and databases.

Let's explore a few examples.

Flow Statement

Like any programming language, Jinja2 provides keywords to control the rendering of resources. Let's investigate different `for` statements that can be used to construct an */etc/hosts* file:

```
{% for host in hosts %} ❶
    {{ host.ip }}    {{ host.hostname }}
{% endfor %}

{% for host in hosts if not 'localhost' == host.hostname %} ❷
    {{ host.ip }}    {{ host.hostname }}
{% endfor %}

{% for host in hosts %}
    {{ host.ip }}    {{ host.hostname }}
{% else %} ❸
    # No hosts configured
{% endfor %}
```

❶ Iterating over a list.

❷ Iterating over a list only if the value is not `localhost`.

❸ In case of an empty list, execute this block.

Macros

In the Jinja2 engine, *macros* are similar to functions in programming languages. Macros let you define fragments that can be reused in other parts of the template:

```
❶
{% macro username(name, surname='') -%}  ❷
    <user>
      <name>{{name|e}}</name> ❸
      <surname>{{surname|e}}</surname>
    </user>
{%- endmacro %}

<users>
{{ username('Ada', 'Soto') }} ❹
{{ username('Alexandra', 'Soto') }}
</users>
```

❶ Defines the macro with the parameters

❷ Sets a parameter with a default value

❸ `|e` escapes special characters

❹ Calls the macro

The resulting XML file after applying the template is:

```
<users>
  <user>
    <name>Ada</name>
    <surname>Soto</surname>
  </user>
  <user>
    <name>Alexandra</name>
    <surname>Soto</surname>
  </user>
</users>
```

Include

The include tag renders another template and outputs the result into the current template:

```
{% include 'db.properties.j2' %} ❶
{% include 'security.properties.j2' %}
port = 8082
```

❶ Includes the given template

Blocks

Blocks are used for inheritance; you define a base template with some empty sections, and the inherited blocks define the content of the empty sections. Let's define a base firewalld configuration file with two sections or blocks that will be completed by a child template:

```
<zone>
  <short>My Zone</short>
  <description>Here you can describe the characteristic features of the zone.
  </description>
  <service name="{% block service %}{% endblock %}"/> ❶
  {% block port %}{% endblock %}
</zone>
```

❶ Defines an empty block with the name service

A child template completing the firewall configuration for the SSH service is shown in this snippet:

```
{% extends "firewalld_base.xml" %}
{% block service %}ssh{% endblock %} ❶
{% block port %} ❷
  <port protocol="udp" port="1025-65535"/>
```

```
    <port protocol="tcp" port="1025-65535"/>
{% endblock %}
```

1. Sets the service name

2. Adds a block with multiple lines

Blocks can also be used to reuse templates.

Filters

Filters (*https://oreil.ly/VtxBH*) are a way to modify the variable's value. For example, you can use filters to escape characters, capitalize a string, eliminate HTML tags, or reverse the content.

A pipe symbol (|) invokes filters from the variable and may have optional arguments in parentheses. Multiple filters can be chained together to create a powerful pipeline of actions.

Let's see some filter examples:

```
{{html|escape}} ❶
{{html|striptags|capitalize}} ❷
{{config}|pprint} ❸
{{listHosts|join('-')}} ❹
```

1. Calls the `escape` filter to replace the characters to be compatible with HTML-safe sequences

2. Chains two filters together to remove tags and capitalize the result

3. Pretty prints a variable. Useful for debugging

4. Calls the `join` filter that requires a parameter that will combine multiple strings and separate their values with the content of the separator

Lookup

Ansible includes several lookup plug-ins that can be used to retrieve content from external resources, such as a file or URL. These lookup plug-ins are similar to templates, and Ansible executes and evaluates them on the Ansible control machine (local machine).

Lookup plug-ins can be used anywhere you can use templating in Ansible; for example, in a play, a variables file, or a Jinja2 template.

Let's use `lookup` to populate a variable with the content of the */etc/hosts* file (located on your local machine):

```
- name: Read
  hosts: all
  vars:
    hosts_value: "{{ lookup('file', '/etc/hosts') }}" ❶
  tasks:
  - debug:
      msg: "hosts value is {{ hosts_value }}"
```

❶ Sets the content of the local file as the `hosts_value` variable

If this file is not present on the local machine, an error will occur.

Similarly, `lookup` can be used in a template. For example, we can use a `lookup` to retrieve properties from a remote file and append the content into the rendered template.

The remote file that will be created is a configuration file and contains two properties:

```
connectionpool=50
url=jdbc:h2:~/test
```

To inject this remote file into the template, use the `lookup` method with the `url` plug-in:

```
hostname={{ ansible_hostname }}

{{ lookup('url', 'https://bit.ly/4lj0wHb') }}
```

Ansible renders this template into the following file:

```
hostname=localhost

connectionpool=50,url=jdbc:h2:~/test
```

This is because `url` returns all the content as a single line separated by commas.

Set the `split_lines` parameter to `false` to respect line breaks. Rewrite the lookup to `lookup('url', 'https://bit.ly/4lj0wHb', split_lines=False)`.

Apart from the `split_lines` parameter, the `wantlist` parameter can be used to return the content explicitly as a list, which is a perfect match when you want to loop through the returned results.

All of the available lookup plugins are listed on Ansible (*https://oreil.ly/snRKp*).

Conclusion

In this chapter, you've learned about copying and managing files from the control node to managed nodes. Moreover, you saw the importance of using templates to reduce the boilerplate code in Ansible.

It's time to take this Ansible knowledge to the next level by learning how to develop custom modules when none of the existing modules match your requirements.

CHAPTER 7

Module Development

So far, we have defined tasks that ultimately end up executing some type of operation in the local (control) or remote (managed) hosts. These operations invoke modules. So far in this book, you have already used a variety of modules without knowing it. For example, you used the `ansible.builtin.file` (or `file` in short form) module to create a directory on the remote host. You have also used other file-related modules to copy a file from the local host to the remote host.

In this chapter, we will cover in detail what modules are, how to retrieve their associated documentation, and finally, how to develop a new module.

What Is a Module?

Ansible modules are standalone scripts that execute one specific action.

Ansible modules let Ansible developers abstract complexity and provide Ansible users with an easier way to execute automation tasks without needing to be concerned with the actions being performed. For instance, as a developer, when using the `template` module, you do not need to worry about writing tooling to utilize the Jinja2 engine to render content or set the variables for any of the included placeholders. All you need are the required parameters that the `template` module supports. For example:

```
- name: Copy conf files
  ansible.builtin.template:
    src: "conf.properties.j2"
    dest: "/tmp/conf.properties"
```

The code snippet does not include any details about Jinja2 or how the files are going to be rendered using the framework. All you need to do is set two parameters, and the module does the rest.

Even though modules can be written in any programming language, the majority of modules are written in Python since Ansible itself is written using the language. PowerShell is the other primary module programming language; it is used by modules targeting the Windows operating system. All modules return JSON-format data. Modules should be idempotent and avoid making any changes if they detect that the current state matches the desired final state.

Ansible includes a default set of modules. You can install new ones either by copying them in a directory called *library* or within an Ansible Content Collection.

Ansible Doc

One of the essential tools in Ansible is `ansible-doc`. The tool displays a variety of information related to modules installed in Ansible libraries. Some details that it can provide include short module descriptions, a printout of a modules' `DOCUMENTATION` strings, and a brief "snippet" that can be pasted into a playbook.

Listing Modules

You can list all of the discovered modules within Ansible libraries, with a short description, by running the following command:

```
ansible-doc -l
```

Getting Module Documentation

To retrieve information from a specific module, append the name of the module as the first argument of the `ansible-doc` command:

```
ansible-doc ansible.builtin.git
```

The documentation provided within the module is returned:

```
ANSIBLE.BUILTIN.GIT    (/Library/Python/3.9/lib/python/site-packages/ansible/
modules/git.py)

        Manage `git' checkouts of repositories to deploy files or software.

ADDED IN: version 0.0.1 of ansible-core

OPTIONS (= is mandatory):

- accept_hostkey
        Will ensure or not that "-o StrictHostKeyChecking=no" is present as an
        ssh option.
...
REQUIREMENTS:  git>=1.7.1 (the command line tool)

AUTHOR: Ansible Core Team, Michael DeHaan
```

```
EXAMPLES:

- name: Git checkout
  ansible.builtin.git:
    repo: 'https://foosball.example.org/path/to/repo.git'
    dest: /srv/checkout
    version: release-0.22
...
```

> You can use the fully qualified name or the short name. In the previous case, either `git` or `ansible.builtin.git` could be used.

Now that we have a better understanding of Ansible modules, when they are used, and how they are used, it's time to develop your first module.

Developing Modules

A module is a reusable, standalone script that Ansible runs on your behalf, either in the control or managed nodes.

A module accepts arguments and returns information to Ansible by printing a JSON string to stdout or stderr in the event of error prior to exiting. Since Ansible reads the output produced from a module, it can be developed in any programming language. Ansible itself is written in Python, and the `module_utils` library, which includes many of the standardized functions for Ansible modules, like argument processing, logging, and response writing, among other things, is also written in this language.

Preparing the Directory

When creating a module, you first need to create a directory named *library* inside your workspace directory:

```
mkdir module_example
cd module_example

mkdir library
cd library
```

Let's create an Ansible module that prints a welcome message on a managed host.

Module Code

This new module will print to the host a welcome message consisting of the word *hello* and the name that is provided as a parameter. Moreover, it will return to the control node a JSON document with the status of the invocation.

Four unique variables in a module are used for documentation purposes:

`ANSIBLE_METADATA`
: Information about the plug-in, such as the version, status, or author.

`DOCUMENTATION`
: The module documentation.

`EXAMPLES`
: Provides some examples of using the module.

`RETURN`
: Explains the module's return content.

To get started, create a method named `run_module()`, which is the starting point of the module.

Create a new file named *hello.py* containing the module code:

```
#!/usr/bin/env python ❶

ANSIBLE_METADATA = {
    'metadata_version': '1.0',
    'status': ['preview'],
    'supported_by': 'community'
}

❷
DOCUMENTATION = '''
---
module: demo_hello
short_description: A module that says hello
version_added: "2.8"
description:
  - "A module that says hello."
options:
    name:
        description:
          - Name of the person to salute. If no value is provided the default
            value will be used.
        required: false
        type: str
        default: John Doe
author:
    - The Ops team
```

```
'''

EXAMPLES = '''
# Pass in a custom name
- name: Say hello to Linus Torvalds
  demo_hello:
    name: "Linus Torvalds"
'''

RETURN = '''
fact:
  description: Hello string
  type: str
  sample: Hello John Doe!
'''

❸
from ansible.module_utils.basic import AnsibleModule


FACTS = "Hello {name}!"


def run_module():
    module_args = dict(
        name=dict(type='str', default='Ada'),
    ) ❹

    module = AnsibleModule(
        argument_spec=module_args,
        supports_check_mode=True
    ) ❺

    result = dict(
        changed=False,
        fact=''
    ) ❻

    txt=FACTS.format(name=module.params['name']) ❼

    println(txt)

    result['fact'] = txt

    if module.check_mode:
        return result

    module.exit_json(**result) ❽


def main():
    run_module()
```

```
if __name__ == '__main__':
    main()
```

❶ Sets the path to the runtime

❷ Defines the variables used by the `ansible-doc` tool

❸ Imports `AnsibleModule` that includes a number of helper utilities

❹ Parses input parameters

❺ Instantiates an `AnsibleModule`

❻ Prepares the output content

❼ Gets the `name` argument and uses it to create the message

❽ Returns the result

Using the Module

To use this module, go to the parent directory, in this example, the *module_example* directory, and create a playbook file called *playbook.yaml* with the following content:

```
- name: CustomModule
  hosts: all

  tasks:
    - name: executes custom module
      hello: ❶
        name: "Alexandra" ❷
      register: demo_greeting
    - name: dump output
      ansible.builtin.debug:
        msg: "{{ demo_greeting }}\n"
```

❶ The module name is the name of the file containing the module code without the extension.

❷ This sets the argument of the module.

Executing the Playbook

There are four ways to enable custom modules in a playbook:

- They can be copied into any directory added to the `ANSIBLE_LIBRARY` environment variable (for multiple locations, use a colon [`:`] between each location).
- They can be copied into *~/.ansible/plugins/modules/*.
- They can be copied into */usr/share/ansible/plugins/modules/*.
- They can be copied into a collection.

In our case, set the `ANSIBLE_LIBRARY` environment variable to the *library* directory.

To run the playbook, execute the following command:

```
ANSIBLE_LIBRARY=./library ansible-playbook -i inventory playbook.yaml
```

The output shows the output of the module:

```
TASK [dump output] ***
ok: [192.168.1.115] => {
    "msg": {
        "changed": false,
        "fact": "Hello Alexandra!",
        "failed": false
    }
}
```

The output is the JSON document created in the module filled with the values from the invocation.

Conclusion

So far, you've seen how to develop and run a module. To share a module, you can upload it to a repository and download it before using it on all machines where Ansible is run.

In the following chapter, you will learn a more convenient way to share modules with Ansible roles and collections.

CHAPTER 8

Ansible Roles and Collections

Throughout the book, you have seen how to write playbooks to execute specific tasks. For example, we have covered tasks such as copying files into managed servers, creating users, manipulating files, or installing packages (such as the Java Virtual Machine). But what happens when you need to reuse the same tasks through different projects?

Do you remember one of the first examples in the book, where we reviewed a complete playbook for deploying an ngnix service? The steps included in the playbook covered:

1. Install nginx.
2. Configure nginx.
3. Copy the HTML file to the appropriate directory to publish the web page.
4. Restart nginx to have the configuration changes applied.
5. Test that the web page is correctly published.
6. Configure the firewall.

As you can imagine, this process can be repeated for any ngnix project. How can you share this playbook among other projects so they don't need to repeat the development of the same playbook over and over again?

In this chapter, we will cover Ansible roles and collections, important parts of the Ansible ecosystem that allow you to package custom Ansible content, including modules and playbooks, and share them across your organization.

Ansible Roles

When using Ansible, a playbook includes a series of tasks that accomplish an automation goal. But, at some point, when your level of automation is mature enough, you will begin to wonder how to best structure and share these playbooks with others.

The answer to this question is Ansible roles. Ansible roles provide a standard structure for declaring tasks, variables, templates, handlers, or modules. Because all the components follow a well-known structure, Ansible code is cleaner and more maintainable as all of the components follow a well-known structure. Roles are also distributable, as you can package and share the contents with others.

Moreover, Ansible roles are parameterizable. For example, when a Java application is installed on a managed host, this might require some specific parameters (like heap memory or garbage collector configuration) that might be different in another host. When calling an Ansible role from a playbook, you only need to invoke the role along with a series of optional parameters. The tasks implemented within the role are executed with the given parameters.

Another example of an Ansible role is installing a PostgreSQL server for any application that requires a PostgreSQL database.

Before developing an Ansible role and seeing the directory layout of a role, let's introduce Ansible Galaxy.

Downloading Roles from Ansible Galaxy

Ansible Galaxy (*https://galaxy.ansible.com*) provides community prepackaged Ansible roles and collections that can be used within Ansible automation (Figure 8-1). It provides similar functionality as Maven Central or PyPi as a way to share and consume Ansible roles (and collections).

At the beginning of the book, you installed the Java Virtual Machine (JVM) using the `dnf` module. Using this module is one way of accomplishing the installation of a package, but using an Ansible role simplifies the steps you need to take within your automation to install and configure Java. Let's install Java using an Ansible role available from Ansible Galaxy.

Ansible includes the `ansible-galaxy` tool to manage artifacts hosted on Ansible Galaxy.

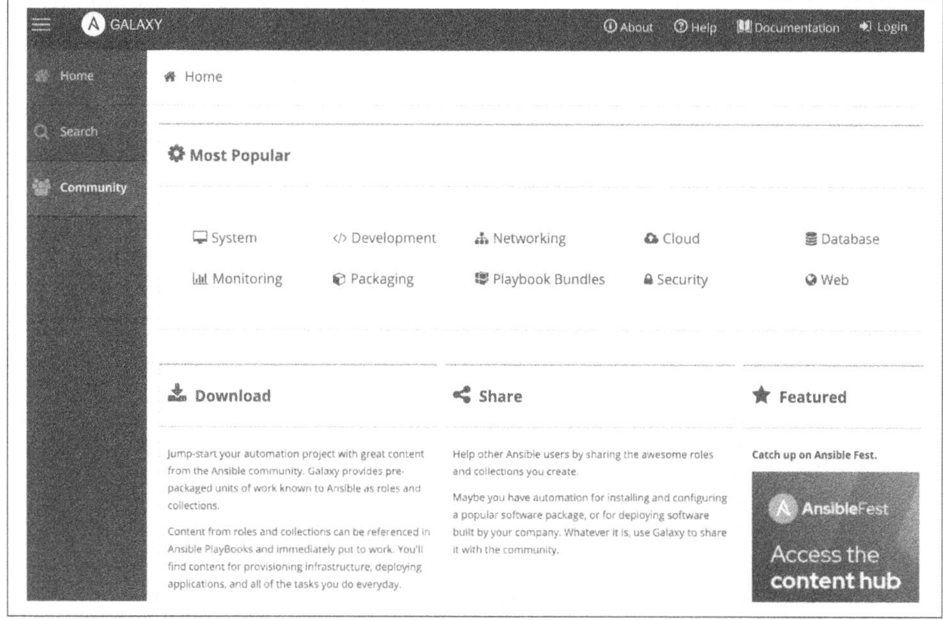

Figure 8-1. Ansible Galaxy home

An Example of a Role

The `geerlingguy.java` is an Ansible role (*https://oreil.ly/Htqt3*) used to manage the JVM installations. Figure 8-2 shows a screenshot of the Ansible Galaxy for this role.

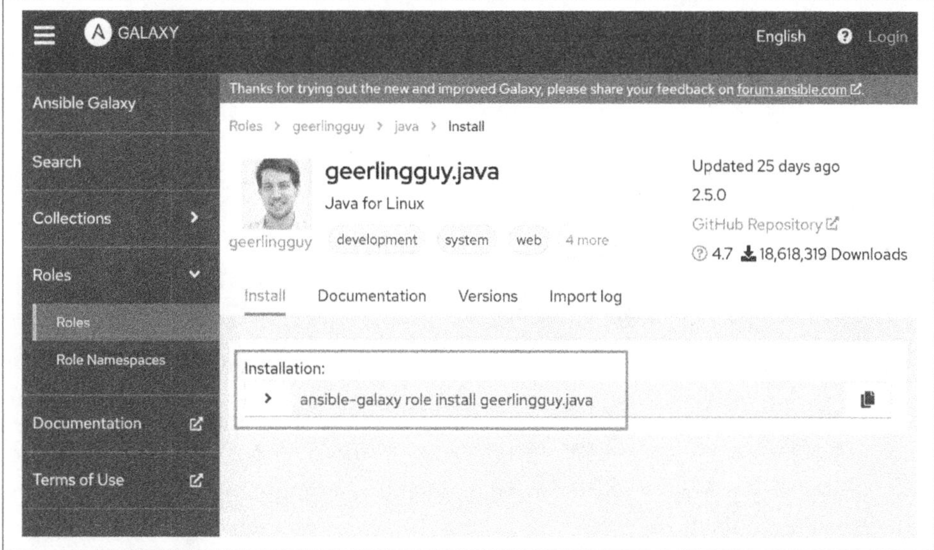

Figure 8-2. Ansible Galaxy Java role

As you can see, Ansible Galaxy looks like a portal for Ansible roles and collections, providing information about how to install versions of published artifacts and view associated documentation.

Figure 8-3 shows a screenshot of the documentation for the Java role.

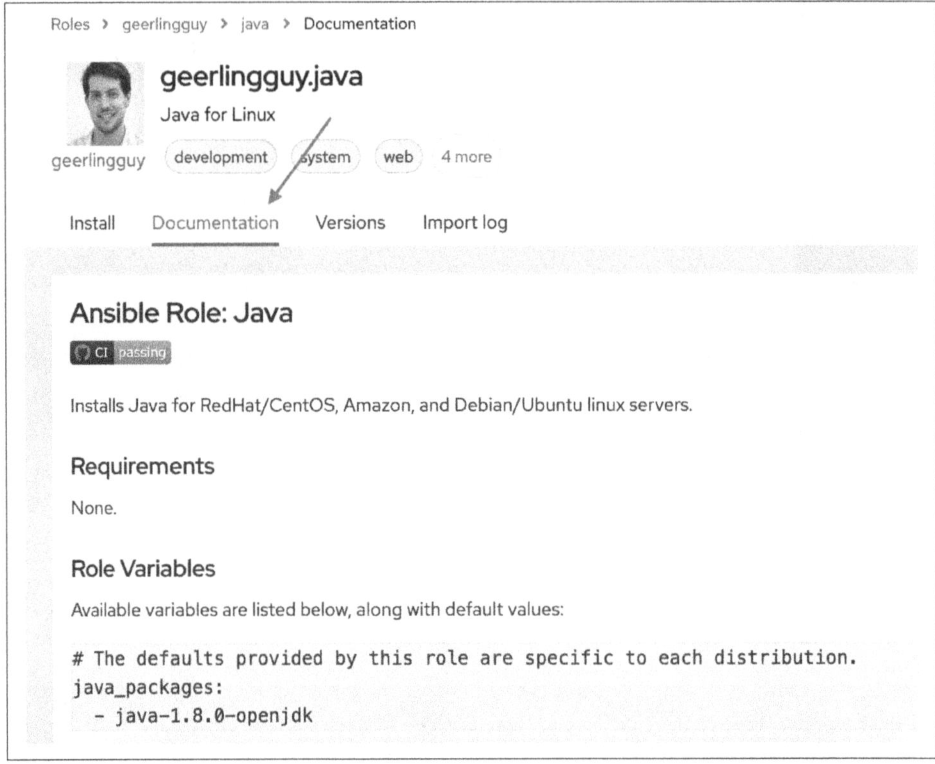

Figure 8-3. Ansible Java role documentation

To install the Ansible role into the control node, open a terminal window and run the following command:

```
ansible-galaxy install geerlingguy.java

Starting galaxy role install process
- downloading role 'java', owned by geerlingguy
- downloading Role from https://github.com/geerlingguy/ansible-role-java/
archive/2.2.0.tar.gz
- extracting geerlingguy.java to /<>/.ansible/roles/geerlingguy.java
- geerlingguy.java (2.2.0) was installed successfully
```

The Java Ansible role is installed on the node and can be used within a playbook or other Ansible automation.

Using a Role in a Playbook

To use this role, create a playbook named *playbook-jdk.yml*. The `roles` section registers and configures the Java role execution, and sets the `java_packages` property to `java-1.8.0-openjdk`:

```
- hosts: all
  become: true
  roles: ❶
  - role: geerlingguy.java ❷
    when: "ansible_os_family == 'RedHat'" ❸
    vars:
      java_packages: ❹
        - java-1.8.0-openjdk ❺
```

❶ `roles` section to set the list of roles to execute

❷ The name of the role that should be invoked

❸ A conditional that determines when the role should be invoked

❹ Parameter name

❺ Parameter value

Let's execute this playbook to see roles in action:

```
ansible-playbook -i inventory playbook-jdk.yaml
```

The execution is done through a playbook; the only thing to keep in mind is to download the role.

The output should be similar to the following:

```
PLAY [all]

TASK [Gathering Facts]
ok: [production]

TASK [geerlingguy.java : Include OS-specific variables for Fedora or FreeBSD.]
ok: [production]

TASK [geerlingguy.java : Define java_packages.]
skipping: [production]

TASK [geerlingguy.java : include_tasks]
included: /Users/<>/.ansible/roles/geerlingguy.java/tasks/setup-RedHat.yml for
staging, production

TASK [geerlingguy.java : Ensure Java is installed.]
changed: [production]
```

```
TASK [geerlingguy.java : include_tasks]
skipping: [production]

TASK [geerlingguy.java : include_tasks]
skipping: [production]

TASK [geerlingguy.java : Set JAVA_HOME if configured.]
skipping: [production]
```

After executing this playbook, all hosts defined in the *inventory* file will have installed Java 1.8.0. Notice that everything is much simpler (and cleaner) now. All that is needed is to specify the name of the role and the Java version you want to install. The role will detect the operating system and install the Java version using the corresponding package manager (`apt-get`, `dnf`, etc.).

What's important to note here is the number of tasks executed under the covers, such as installing Java, verifying the installation, and configuring any required properties (`JAVA_HOME`). But you, as an Ansible developer, only need to set a few lines in your automation.

The incorporation of roles in the playbook abstracts you from implementation details and enables reuse within multiple operating systems, including any project that needs to have Java installed.

Order of Execution

When mixing `roles` and `tasks` sections in a playbook, the execution order of steps is as follows.

First, Ansible runs each role listed in the `roles` section in the order listed. Any role dependencies defined in the *meta/main.yml* of a role are executed first and are subject to tag filtering and conditionals. Once complete, any tasks described in the play are then executed.

This is the default behavior. While it is straightforward, there are some limitations such as running roles between tasks. Specify a task and call the `include_role` or `import_role` module within a task to not suffer from the same limitations as described previously. This also offers further options to customize how the role is executed.

The following snippet executes the `geerlingguy.java` role within the list of tasks using the `include_role` module:

```
- hosts: all
  become: true
  tasks:
    - name: Install JDK
      ansible.builtin.include_role: ❶
```

```
      name: geerlingguy.java ❷
    vars: ❸
      java_packages: ❹
        - java-1.8.0-openjdk
```

❶ Invokes the role

❷ Name of the role

❸ Defines the variable values for the role

❹ Specifies the `java_packages` role parameter containing the list of packages to install

So far, you learned how to search for and download roles from Ansible Galaxy as well as use them in a playbook. In the following section, you will learn how to develop a role of your own.

Developing a Role

There are many roles readily available for use within Ansible Galaxy that might fit your requirements. However, there may be reasons, such as an organizational policy or a need for a finer level of control, to develop a custom role. Let's develop a simple role that prints the content of a remote file.

You will create a role that combines two tasks:

- Get the content of a file and store the result in a variable.
- Get the `builtin.debug` module that prints out the value.

Moreover, the role will have a parameter to set the file's location.

Scaffolding the Role

Use the `ansible-galaxy` CLI to scaffold the directory layout for the role. Create a new role called `printfile` by running the following command in the terminal window to scaffold the directory layout for the role:

```
ansible-galaxy role init printfile
```

Enter the *printfile* directory that was created to start developing the role. This directory has the following directory structure:

defaults
: Includes default values for role variables.

files
: Contains static and custom files.

handlers
: A set of handlers that are triggered by tasks of the role.

meta
: Metadata information for the role.

tasks
: A list of tasks to be executed by the role.

templates
: Template files used by tasks of the role.

tests
: Assets related to role testing.

vars
: Variables defined for the role.

The primary directory within a role that you will be most concerned with is the *tasks* directory. It is similar to the task section of a playbook, containing YAML files with task definitions.

Implementing the Role

Open the *tasks/main.yml* file and define two tasks: one to execute the `cat` command from a parametrized file and another to debug the file content:

```
- name: Display file contents
  ansible.builtin.command: "cat {{show_file}}" ❶
  register: command_output
- name: Print to console ❷
  ansible.builtin.debug:
    msg: "{{command_output.stdout}}"
```

❶ Retrieves file content from the file indicated in the `show_file` variable

❷ Prints the file content to output

This role uses the `show_file` variable as an input parameter, and it is a good practice to provide default values in case one is not provided by the user. Open the *vars/main.yml* file and include the following content:

```
---
show_file: /etc/hosts
```

In this case, by default, this role prints the remote content of */etc/hosts* as output.

Using the Role

In the previous section, you've seen how to develop a simple role using the `ansible-galaxy install` command. Although this is one way to accomplish the installation of a role, Ansible also supports defining the roles that are needed within a playbook by creating a *requirements.yml* file and populating the contents with all of the required roles.

In the following *requirements.yml* file, you will see everyday use cases for how to declare roles:

```
- name: geerlingguy.java ❶

- src: git+file:///roles/nginx ❷

- name: nginx_role ❸
  src: https://github.com/ansiblebook/nginx
  version: main

- name: myrole
  src: https://some.webserver.example.com/files/myrole.tar.gz ❹
```

❶ Downloads the role from Ansible Galaxy

❷ Uses a local Git repository as the role source

❸ Downloads the role from a Git repository from the `main` branch and sets `ngnix_role` as the role name

❹ Downloads the role from an HTTP server, unpacks the archive, and sets `myrole` as the role name

Usually, this file is created in the *roles* directory as a subdirectory of the playbook location.

Now that the roles have been defined in the *requirements.yml* file, use the `ansible-galaxy` CLI to install them. For example, to install roles defined in a *requirements.yml* file located in *roles/requirements.yml*, execute `ansible-galaxy role install -r roles/requirements.yml`.

Now, let's use the `printfile` role in a playbook. To not overcomplicate, let's create a *tar.gz* file of the role and set it into the *requirements.yml* file. But of course, any other method explained above is valid too.

At the terminal, run the following command one level up from the *printfile* role directory:

```
tar -czvf printfile.tar.gz printfile
```

With the role archive, you can reference it in the *requirements.yml* file.

In a new directory, create a *roles* directory containing a *requirements.yml* file referencing the archive containing the `printfile` role:

```
- name: printfile
  src: file://.../printfile.tar.gz ❶
```

❶ Location of the `printfile` role (i.e., */home/dev/roles/printfile*)

The next step is to create a playbook in the parent of the *roles* directory that was just created so that it can invoke the required role:

```
- hosts: all
  become: true
  tasks:
  - name: Print Hosts
    ansible.builtin.include_role:
      name: printfile ❶
```

❶ Name of the role to invoke from the playbook. Use the name set in the `name` parameter of the *requirements.yml* file.

The last step is downloading the role using the `ansible-galaxy` command and specifying the location of the *requirements.yml* file. Execute the following command within the terminal:

```
ansible-galaxy role install -r roles/requirements.yml
```

It's important to note that the *requirements.yml* file in this case contains a reference to a local role, but it could also contain a reference to an external role stored in a Git repository or from a remote URL.

With all of the steps now complete, you can run the playbook that will invoke the `printfile` role:

```
ansible-playbook -i inventory playbook.yml
```

Ansible roles support handlers to run operations on change, for example, restarting a service when a task changes a configuration file. Let's slightly rewrite the previous role to add one handler.

Handlers in Roles

Now, you'll move the `debug` part as a handler, so Ansible executes the `debug` part when you explicitly notify. Open the *handlers/main.yml* file and include the following content to define the handler in the role:

```
- name: Print to console
  ansible.builtin.debug:
    msg: "{{command_output.stdout}}"
```

The last part is to modify the task to use the handler. Open the *tasks/main.yml* file again and change the debug section to trigger the handler:

```
---
- name: Display file contents
  ansible.builtin.command: "cat {{show_file}}"
  register: command_output
  notify: Print to console
```

Notice that you can reuse this handler in any task defined in the role, making everything more reusable and maintainable.

Before finishing the role section, let's see how to share a role.

Sharing a Role

Now that the role has been developed and tested locally, you might wonder how it can be shared with others. Several options are available, and they lean on the methods provided by the `src` field of the *requirements.yml* file. You could share your roles via any of the following options:

- Git repository
- Ansible Galaxy
- HTTP server

For enterprise solutions and the scope of this book, the best solution might be the Git repository because you can have the code secured, versioned, and stored persistently.

Another valid option is using Ansible Galaxy/Automation Hub, as they offer a central repository to discover, download, and manage Ansible Content Collections—bundles of modules, plug-ins, roles, and documentation.

Final Notes About Roles

A role has a single responsibility, such as installing the Java Virtual Machine or installing a concrete package, but in some cases, you need to execute more than one operation. For example, in the case of installing the PostgreSQL database, you might need to create an account to run the database, install PostgreSQL, probably create a PostgreSQL user as not root, configure it (network, filesystem, pool), and probably create the database schema.

As you can see, it's not a single task but multiple ones. You can achieve this with a role; but roles might not be the best option for this purpose.

In the following section, we'll look at Ansible collections, a way to implement and run tasks with multiple subtasks correctly, following the Ansible role principles.

Ansible Collections

Ansible collections are a method for distributing various Ansible content as a single unit. Ansible collections include resources such as roles, plug-ins, modules, or playbooks in a structured manner.

To some extent, Ansible collections are like Ansible roles. They can be shared with others, use a well-known structure, and leverage the `ansible-galaxy` CLI for management purposes. However, Ansible collections support more types of content and are easier to manage than Ansible roles. We will see this firsthand in the following sections.

POSIX Ansible Collections

Let's see an example of Ansible collections by using the Ansible POSIX collection. This collection contains several modules, for example, one for managing firewalld, another for SELinux, sysctl, and more.

To explore using collections, we'll install the POSIX collection and use the `at` module to schedule a job using the `at` tool. To install the collection, you can either use `ansible-galaxy` or add an entry to the *requirements.yml* file. From the terminal, you can install the collection by executing the following command:

```
ansible-galaxy collection install ansible.posix
```

Or, to install the collection using a *requirements.yml* file, it can be defined within a `collections` section of the file:

```
collections:
  - name: ansible.posix
```

The same methods for distributing roles also support collections too!

Note that roles and collections can both be defined within the same *requirements.yml* file. However, roles must be defined underneath the `roles:` property instead of being placed at the root level of the file.

To install the collection, execute the following command at the terminal:

```
ansible-galaxy collection install -r requirements.yaml
```

Also, you can copy the Ansible collections in any of the two default lookup paths; by default, Ansible copies in the user-scoped path:

User-scoped path
: */home/<username>/.ansible/collections*

System-scoped path
: */usr/share/ansible/collections*

You can override this by setting the `ANSIBLE_COLLECTIONS_PATHS` environment variable to a new location, or also define it in the *ansible.cfg* configuration file.

To use this collection, let's create a playbook that registers the collection and uses one of the modules that are provided by the collection. To refer to a module defined within a collection, you need to use the fully qualified collection name (FQCN) form `<namespace>.<collection>.<module>`:

```
---
- name: set at command
  hosts: production
  become: yes
  tasks:
    - name: Install at Package ❶
      ansible.builtin.dnf:
        name: at >= 2.4
        state: present
    - name: Schedule a command to execute in 1 minute
      ansible.posix.at: ❷
        command: ls -d / > /tmp/ls.txt
        count: 10
        units: minutes
        unique: yes
```

❶ Installs the `at` package to the host containing the `at` command

❷ Uses the FQCN form (collection name + module)

Executing the playbook will result in scheduling a job on a remote machine. To verify it is working, log in to the managed machine and verify that the */tmp/ls.txt* file exists.

If you need to use an Ansible role defined within a collection, use the FQCN plus the role name to refer to the role. For example, a role named `mongodb_install` stored in the `community.mongodb` collection should be referenced using the `roles` section of a playbook or the `import_roles` section of a task as `community.mongodb.mongodb_install`.

Creating an Ansible Collection

Creating an Ansible collection is similar to creating an Ansible role: the `ansible-galaxy` CLI is used to scaffold the layout of a collection. In a terminal window, run the following command to create a collection named `mycollection` under the `mynamespace` namespace:

```
ansible-galaxy collection init mynamespace.mycollection
```

The structure of a collection is the following:

```
.
└── mynamespace ❶
    └── mycollection ❷
        ├── README.md
        ├── docs ❸
        ├── galaxy.yml ❹
        ├── meta  ❺
        │   └── runtime.yml
        ├── plugins ❻
        │   └── README.md
        └── roles ❼
```

❶ The collection namespace

❷ The collection name

❸ Documentation for the collection

❹ Ansible Galaxy metadata

❺ Additional collection metadata

❻ Contains plug-ins, modules, and `module_utils`

❼ Roles provided by the collection

This is the basic structure of a collection. For example, inside roles (you need to create manually), you could place all the roles bundled inside this collection, each one into its own subdirectory. For example, if you want to develop and bundle a module inside the collection, you should place it in the *plugins/modules/* directory. Or place a role named `hello_msg` into the *roles/hello_msg/* directory.

To prepare and package the collection for distribution, from the collection directory (*mynamespace/mycollection*), run the following command to build the collection and generate a *.tar.gz* file that can be installed locally or distributed for others to consume:

```
ansible-galaxy collection build

Created collection for the  mynamespace.mycollection
at <directory>/mynamespace/collection/mynamespace-mycollection-1.0.0.tar.gz  ❶
```

❶ Version taken from *galaxy.yaml*

By default, the `ansible-galaxy collection build` command uses the current directory as the location for the collection. Instead of using the current directory, another directory can be specified as a parameter within this command.

To use this collection, you can use any of the methods explained in the previous section or use the `install` subcommand of the `ansible-galaxy collection` CLI, which copies the specified archive into the *~/.ansible/collections/ansible_collections* directory so it can be used:

```
ansible-galaxy collection install mynamespace-mycollection-1.0.0.tar.gz

Starting galaxy collection install process
Process install dependency map
Starting collection install process
Installing 'mynamespace.collection:1.0.0' to
'<directory>/.ansible/collections/ansible_collections/mynamespace/mycollection'
mynamespace.collection:1.0.0 was installed successfully
```

Then you invoke any elements bundled inside like any other collection, using the fully qualified collection name and the desired component (like a module or role).

Conclusion

Thus far, we have explored Ansible from the basic first steps of running Ansible modules using the CLI to creating Ansible roles or collections that can be shared across the organization. But there's still a lot more to learn about Ansible! In the next chapter, you will be introduced to the various tools for executing Ansible.

CHAPTER 9

Execution Environments

Consistency is one of the key benefits that is realized when applying automation. By performing tasks in a repeatable fashion, the outcome not only is known, but is expected. As we have seen thus far, Ansible automation relies heavily upon the configuration and content of the control node when executing the automation that we have developed. For Ansible automation to be applied successfully to target hosts, the control node must contain all of the necessary dependencies that are required by the automation activities and can include Ansible Content Collections, Python libraries, and operating system packages. However, managing all of these concerns can be challenging.

In this chapter, we will introduce Ansible Execution Environments as a way to package and distribute consistent automation environments. First, we will look at the challenges that Execution Environments attempt to solve. We will then explore Execution Environments in detail, including their composition and the options that they expose. Then, we will introduce the `ansible-builder` tool that enables the creation of Ansible Execution Environments. Finally, building upon these concepts and tools, we will use the Automation Content Navigator to execute automation in an interactive, but predictable manner to instill confidence regardless of the operating environment. These tools have become the primary method for exploring and running Ansible content, and as a result, their use for exploring and running Ansible content is covered in detail in the EX294 exam. Upon the conclusion of this chapter, you will have not only the tools, but the confidence to develop and execute automation anywhere.

The Basics of Execution Environments

Ansible Automation Execution Environments offer a set of solutions to a series of common challenges in cases where automation activities rely on nondefault dependencies in a multiuser environment. By using containers and their inherent benefits, such as a standardized packaging model and runtime format, as control nodes, a consistent method of executing automation can be achieved regardless of where it operates.

Prior to exploring their composition and overall lifecycle, let's review why Execution Environments are needed in the first place and the solutions that they offer.

The Challenge of Managing Automation Consistently

When developing Ansible Automation, and as you begin to tackle more advanced use cases, you will inevitably need to leverage more complex modules or rely on one or more libraries (such as at the Python or operating system level). How these assets are managed, stored, and run can differ quite dramatically. For example, Python libraries are stored in different locations, depending upon the operating system, and certain components may not be suitable to run at all given the particular environment. Python virtual environments were traditionally used in Ansible Automation as the method for handling Python packages and dependencies. However, when having to create multiple virtual environments for the different types of automation being performed, the management of virtual environments became more complex than any automation being developed.

To alleviate these concerns and more, Ansible Execution Environments were developed as a solution to address three primary areas where complexity exists:

- Software dependencies
- Portability
- Content separation

The use of container technologies simplifies how content is stored and distributed. Because these containers only include the desired set of resources in an Execution Environment as an atomic artifact, the concerns related to managing software dependencies and the separation of assets are mitigated. And, since multiple containers can operate within a single host without conflicting with one another, the manageability and stability of automation execution are simplified.

Finally, since container images can be easily shared and distributed between instances and environments, there is assurance that the same content can be reused wherever it is needed to achieve the same results.

Execution Environment Composition

An Execution Environment is made up of several components working together to provide a suitable environment for automation. A standard Execution Environment contains:

- `ansible-core`
- `ansible-runner`
- Python
- Ansible content dependencies

While the majority of the content included within an Execution Environment contains tooling that we have encountered previously, including `ansible-core` and Python, `ansible-runner` serves an important role within Execution Environments as it provides a common interface that is responsible for running `ansible` and `ansible-playbook` tasks and gathers the results when the execution completes. These activities, for the most part, are abstracted away from the end user. But it is important to understand all of the key components that are included within an Execution Environment, their roles, and how they are used.

An Execution Environment will also include one or more Ansible Content Collections and any dependencies that these collections rely on, as well as any other supporting tool that is needed by the automation (operating system packages, binaries, etc.).

The Ansible Automation Platform includes several base Execution Environment images that can either be used as is or act as the foundation for your own custom Execution Environment:

`ee-minimal`
: Ansible Execution Environment containing the baseline capabilities and features

`ee-supported`
: Ansible Execution Environment containing all of the supported Ansible Content Collections

With an understanding of Ansible Execution Environments, their composition, and the base images available, let's look at what it will take to create an Execution Environment of our own as a suitable environment for our automation activities.

Building Execution Environments

The `ansible-builder` tool automates the process of creating Ansible Execution Environments. It leverages a definition file that enables end users to define key components that an Execution Environment should contain, such as packages for the underlying operating system of the container image, Ansible Content Collections, and Python libraries.

Installing Ansible Builder

There are many ways to install Ansible Builder. However, since Execution Environments make use of container technologies, and Ansible Builder produces a container image, a container runtime, such as Podman or Docker, must be installed. If you completed Chapter 4, "Variables and Host Management", then Docker was previously installed, satisfying the required prerequisites.

Several installation options are available, including:

- Install the release with your OS package manager (`yum` or `dnf`).
- Install with `pip` (the Python package manager).
- Install from source or tarballs.

When using the Fedora or RHEL operating system, you can use `dnf`:

```
sudo dnf install ansible-builder
```

When using a macOS-based system, the preferred installation tool is `pip`:

```
pip install --user ansible-builder
```

Of course, you can also produce a build from source or leverage the tarball releases from the upstream project (*https://oreil.ly/efcHA*).

Once `ansible-builder` has been installed successfully, verify the installation by checking the version of the tool. At the time of this writing, the latest Ansible Builder version is 3.1.0:

```
ansible-builder --version

3.1.0
```

Defining an Execution Environment

The contents of an Execution Environment are declared in a definition file that is provided to the `ansible-builder` utility. This file is YAML formatted and by convention is named *execution-environment.yml*. However, an alternate filename can be provided.

Once the definition file has been created, Ansible Builder reads the content, performs syntactical validation, and generates a Containerfile that shares the same syntax as a Dockerfile. Control is then passed to the container runtime that performs the build and produces the resulting image.

To better understand what it takes to produce an Execution Environment, we will explore, in detail, the various sections within an Execution Environment definition file and the options that enable you to craft the most optimal manifest to suit your use cases.

To begin, review an example of an Execution Environment definition file:

```
version: 3 ❶

build_arg_defaults: ❷
  ANSIBLE_GALAXY_CLI_COLLECTION_OPTS: '--pre'

dependencies: ❸
  galaxy: requirements.yml
  python:
    - six
    - psutil
  system: bindep.txt

images: ❹
  base_image:
    name: "registry.redhat.io/ansible-automation-platform-25/\
      ee-minimal-rhel9:latest"

# Custom package manager path for the RHEL based images
 options: ❺
   package_manager_path: /usr/bin/microdnf

additional_build_steps: ❻
  prepend_base:
    - RUN echo This is a prepend base command!

  prepend_galaxy:
    # Environment variables used for Galaxy client configurations
    - ENV ANSIBLE_GALAXY_SERVER_LIST=automation_hub
    - ENV ANSIBLE_GALAXY_SERVER_AUTOMATION_HUB_URL=https://console.redhat.com/
    api/automation-hub/content/xxxxxxx-synclist/
    - ENV ANSIBLE_GALAXY_SERVER_AUTOMATION_HUB_AUTH_URL=https://sso.redhat.com/
    auth/realms/redhat-external/protocol/openid-connect/token
    # define a custom build arg env passthrough - we still also have to pass
    # `--build-arg ANSIBLE_GALAXY_SERVER_AUTOMATION_HUB_TOKEN` to get it to
    pick it up from the env
    - ARG ANSIBLE_GALAXY_SERVER_AUTOMATION_HUB_TOKEN

  prepend_final: |
    RUN whoami
    RUN cat /etc/os-release
  append_final:
    - RUN echo This is a post-install command!
    - RUN ls -la /etc
```

❶ Execution Environment schema version

❷ Default build arguments

❸ Specifies the location of files that will be used for dependency management

❹ The base image that will be used for the Execution Environment build

❺ Options that affect the functionality of the build

❻ Custom steps at different points in the build process

This example is fairly comprehensive as it illustrates the primary methods for which an Execution Environment can be defined and customized. One of the most important properties is the `version` property, as shown at the top of the example. This property represents a version 3 Execution Environment definition file. This value should be specified so that Ansible Builder will leverage the appropriate capabilities of the tool. Otherwise, version 1 is used, and it is functionally less capable than more recent versions.

To better understand the options available when configuring an Execution Environment definition file, let's break down the top-level properties.

Build arguments

The `build_arg_defaults` contains variables that provide default arguments to the Ansible Builder build. Table 9-1 describes the two properties that can be specified in this section.

Table 9-1. Execution Environment definition file build arguments

Name	Description
`ANSIBLE_GALAXY_CLI_COLLECTION_OPTS`	Arbitrary arguments that are passed to the `ansible-galaxy` CLI as collections are instantiated, such as `-c` which bypasses SSL certificate verification
`ANSIBLE_GALAXY_CLI_ROLE_OPTS`	Flags that are passed as part of role instantiation, such as `-no-deps`

Galaxy

The `galaxy` property within the *dependencies* section includes references to a *requirements* file or explicit declarations for Ansible collections. When specifying the location of a requirements file, the value can either be a path relative to the Execution Environment definition file or an absolute path.

Here is an example of how this property can be specified within an Execution Environment definition file:

```
dependencies:
  galaxy: requirements.yml
```

Alternatively, the desired collections can be defined explicitly within the Execution Environment file:

```
dependencies:
  galaxy:
    collections:
      - ansible.controller
      - community.general
```

Python

The `python` property within the `dependencies` section, similar to the `galaxy` property, specifies the location of a *requirements* or explicit declaration of Python packages in PEP508 format (*https://oreil.ly/8X0n2*) so that it can be used in the `pip install` command.

Examples of valid values that can be included in a requirements file are:

```
packaging
requests>=2.4.2
python-dateutil==2.7.0
```

These values can either be specified within a requirements file:

```
dependencies:
  python: requirements.txt
```

Or explicitly defined within the Execution Environment definition file:

```
dependencies:
  python:
    - packaging
```

System

Similar to the other properties defined in the `dependencies` section, the `system` property specifies the set of binary packages in bindep format (*https://oreil.ly/oM3Gy*). This allows for operating system software packages to be installed within the Execution Environment. This property is important, as Execution Environments may rely on features that are provided by the underlying operating system and are not provided by either Ansible or the Python programming language.

The bindep definitions can either be specified in a requirements file or declared in the Execution Environment definition file. The following is an example of how packages can be declared explicitly:

```
dependencies:
  system:
    - iputils
```

Images

Execution Environments that are produced using Ansible Builder extend content provided by an existing container image. The `base_image` property within the `images` section allows for the location of the image to be specified:

```
images:
  base_image:
    name: "registry.redhat.io/ansible-automation-platform-25/\
      ee-minimal-rhel9:latest"
```

If this value is not provided, when Ansible Builder is installed from a Red Hat RPM repository, as of version 3.1.0, the default base image is *registry.redhat.io/ansible-automation- platform-24/ee-minimal-rhel8:latest.*

Additional build files

Within the `additional_build_files` property, arbitrary files can be sourced into the build context. This section contains a list of dictionary values that allow for the file's origin location, using the `src` property, and the destination where the file should be placed within the build context, using the `dest` property. For example:

```
additional_build_files:
  - src: ansible.cfg
    dest: configs
```

The most common use case for this capability, as shown in this example, is the ability to leverage a custom *ansible.cfg* file, which should be used within the resulting Execution Environment image.

Additional custom build steps

The process of producing an Execution Environment using Ansible Builder occurs in several distinct stages:

base
: Customizations of key base image components, such as `pip` and `ansible-core`

galaxy
: Ansible collections, Python, and operating system packages downloaded and stored for later phases

builder
: Python dependencies declared by collections are merged with those downloaded and stored previously to produce a final set of Python packages, which are in turn stored for later phases

final
: Previously downloaded collections, Python, and operating system packages are installed

Additional actions (Containerfile directives) can be specified to achieve greater control over the build process. The list of options that can be configured within the `additional_build_steps` property in the Execution Environment definition file are described in Table 9-2.

Table 9-2. Additional build steps

Value	Description
`prepend_base`	Commands to insert before building the base image
`append_base`	Commands to insert after building the base image
`prepend_galaxy`	Commands to insert before building the galaxy image
`append_galaxy`	Commands to insert after building the galaxy image
`prepend_builder`	Commands to insert before building the Python builder image
`append_builder`	Commands to insert after building the Python builder image
`prepend_final`	Commands to insert before building the final image

Support is available for defining commands as either a multiline string or a list.

The following code demonstrates how to inject custom commands into multiple phases of the build process to upgrade the PIP package manager before building the base image, and how to copy an *ansible.cfg* file that was specified as an additional build file to the default location within the */etc/ansible* directory prior to downloading Ansible Galaxy collections:

```
additional_build_steps:
  append_base:
    - RUN $PYCMD -m pip install -U pip
  prepend_galaxy:
    - COPY _build/configs/ansible.cfg /etc/ansible/ansible.cfg
```

With an understanding of the various options available for customizing an Execution Environment definition file, let's create an Execution Environment image of our own. This image will contain the `community.general` collection and a Python dependency to enable the use of modules within the collection.

Create a new directory called *ee-build* and then change into the directory:

```
mkdir ee-build
cd ee-build
```

Now, create an *execution-environment.yml* file with the following contents:

```
version: 3
```

```
build_arg_defaults:
  ANSIBLE_GALAXY_CLI_COLLECTION_OPTS: '--pre'

dependencies:
  galaxy:
    collections:
      - community.general
  python:
    - jmespath
```

With the created *execution-environment.yml* definition file, an Execution Environment image can be created.

Performing an Execution Environment Build

A prepared Execution Environment definition file can be processed using the `ansible-builder` utility. To produce an Execution Environment image using Ansible Builder, two steps occur:

1. The Execution Environment definition file is rendered, producing a Containerfile with the steps necessary to produce the final image, along with any additional build artifacts.
2. The Containerfile is built using the specified container runtime, resulting in a Execution Environment image.

These steps can be decoupled from one another, so if you needed to forego the actual build of the container image, as described in step 2, this could be achieved.

To render the Containerfile without building the image, use the `ansible-builder create` command. From within the directory containing the *execution-environment.yml* file, render the Containerfile, as shown below:

```
ansible-builder create
```

The `ansible-builder create` command creates a build *context* that, by default, is created within a directory called `context`. This location can be changed by passing the `-c` command. Aside from the Containerfile, several other file resources are also populated, including any dependencies and any other components to support the build process:

```
.
├── context
│   ├── _build
│   │   ├── requirements.txt
│   │   ├── requirements.yml
│   │   └── scripts
│   │       ├── assemble
│   │       ├── check_ansible
│   │       ├── check_galaxy
```

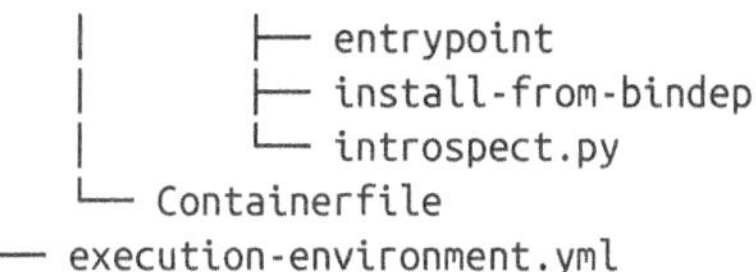

│ │ ├── entrypoint
│ │ ├── install-from-bindep
│ │ └── introspect.py
│ └── Containerfile
└── execution-environment.yml

Once the build context has been created, the designated container runtime, Podman or Docker, can be used to build the image directly from the rendered Containerfile. However, the preferred method of building an Execution Environment image is to use Ansible Builder and the `ansible-builder build` command.

Podman is the default container runtime that is used by Ansible Navigator and will be introduced in the following section. The `--ce` option can be used to specify the Container Engine.

The `ansible-builder build` command can also be used to perform the steps achieved by the `ansible-builder create` command, so there is no need to explicitly invoke this command if the goal is to produce an Execution Environment image.

We will now build an Execution Environment image using the `ansible-builder build` command. While several flags are available to customize the build process, the `-t` flag specifies the name of the image that should be produced. Create a new Execution Environment image with the tag `localhost/ee-build:latest` from within the *ee-build* directory by executing the following command:

```
ansible-builder build -t localhost/ee-build:latest
```

Base images that originate from protected registries, such as the Red Hat Container Catalog, require authentication at container runtime. If you do not have access to the Red Hat Container Catalog, the Red Hat Developer Program includes a no-cost Red Hat Enterprise Linux Developer Subscription (*https://developers.redhat.com*) that can be used to access protected images. To authenticate against protected container images, use `podman login` when using Podman as the container engine to facilitate the authentication process.

Once the build process completes, the image can be found within the container runtime and is eligible for use. Like any other container image, the Execution Environment image can be published to a container registry, like quay.io, so that it can be made available to others. The image can also be published to the Ansible Private Automation Hub so that it can be managed within the Ansible Automation Platform. More information related to the Private Automation Hub can be found within the official product documentation.

With an Execution Environment now available, it can be used within automation activities. In the next section, you will be introduced to Ansible Navigator, a tool for exploring and executing automation content.

Automation Content Navigator

Ansible can be run in a variety of ways and on many different platforms—from a developer's machine that can host several different operating systems, to an automation environment, such as the Ansible Automation Platform. To avoid some of the challenges that Ansible creators previously experienced, Automation Content Navigator (Ansible Navigator) was developed as a tool that provides a seamless method of developing and executing automation.

Automation Content Navigator is a command-line tool as well as a text-based user interface (TUI) for managing Ansible content. This enables you to:

- Launch jobs and playbooks
- Explore Automation Execution Environments
- Browse inventories
- View module documentation

Installing Automation Content Navigator

Automation Content Navigator and its (`ansible-navigator`) CLI can be installed using several different methods:

- Install the release with your OS package manager (`yum` or `dnf`).
- Install with `pip` (the Python package manager).
- Install from source or tarballs.

When using the Fedora or RHEL operating system, `dnf` can be used:

```
sudo dnf install ansible-navigator
```

When using a macOS-based system, the preferred installation tool is `pip`:

```
pip install --user ansible-navigator
```

Automation Content Navigator can also be installed either by producing a build from source or leveraging the tarball releases from the upstream project (*https://oreil.ly/tYGW9*).

After `ansible-navigator` has been installed, verify that the installation was successful by checking the version of the tool. At the time of this writing, the latest Ansible Builder version is 24.9.0:

```
ansible-navigator --version

24.9.0
```

Working with Automation Content Navigator

`ansible-navigator` operates in two modes (stdout and text-based user interface), controlled by the `-m` flag:

stdout mode
: The traditional command-line interface experience. Ansible commands and options can be specified as command-line options.

Text-based user interface mode
: An enhanced method of working with Ansible commands that provides an interactive experience compatible with Integrated Development Environments (IDEs), including Visual Code Studio.

This mode has several options from a user interface perspective, including:

Colon commands
: Commands can be accessed with a colon, such as `:run` or `:collections`.

Navigation
: A dedicated screen describes how to move around, including paging up or down, scrolling, or returning to a previous screen with the Esc key.

Output by line number
: This makes it easy to access to any line number provided in the output, such as `:14`.

Color-coded output
: Colorized output based on the content.

Pagination and scrolling
: You can move around the screen with options provided at the bottom of the screen.

Automation Content Navigator commands

Multiple Ansible related subcommands are exposed by Automation Content Navigator. These commands not only expose capabilities but are primarily aligned to some of the other tools in the Ansible ecosystem. Table 9-3 describes the subcommands available.

Table 9-3. Automation content navigator subcommands

Command	Description	Ansible CLI command
`builder`	Build an Execution Environment image	`ansible-builder`
`collections`	Explore available collections	`ansible-galaxy collection`
`config`	Explore the current Ansible configuration	`ansible-config`
`doc`	Review module or plug-in documentation	`ansible-doc`
`exec`	Run a command within the Execution Environment	N/A
`images`	Explore Execution Environment images	N/A
`inventory`	Explore an inventory	`ansible-inventory`
`lint`	Lint a file or directory	`ansible-lint`
`replay`	Explore a previous playbook run from an artifact	N/A
`run`	Execute a playbook	`ansible-playbook`
`settings`	Automation Content Navigator settings	N/A
`welcome`	Display the Welcome page	N/A

The `ansible-navigator --help` or `ansible-navigator <subcommand> --help` commands provide a detailed set of available options.

Automation Content Navigator basics

The best way to get started with the Ansible CLI is in TUI mode, as it provides an interactive experience for end users. The majority of the activities that occur in Automation Content Navigator leverage an Automation Execution Environment as a runtime. The `--eei` option is used to specify an alternate Execution Environment image, such as the one produced in the previous section.

The default Execution Environment image used in Automation Content Navigator is `registry.redhat.io/ansible-automation-platform-25/ee-supported-rhel8:latest`.

This command launches `ansible-navigator` in TUI mode:

```
ansible-navigator
```

The default Execution Environment image will be pulled and used as the operating environment for subsequent activities. The Welcome screen will be displayed, indicating the available options:

```
 0|Welcome
 1|——————————————————————————————————————————————————————————————————————————————
 2|
 3|Some things you can try from here:
 4|- :collections                        Explore available collections
 5|- :config                             Explore the current ansible configuration
 6|- :doc <plugin>                       Review documentation for a module or
plugin
 7|- :help                              Show the main help page
 8|- :images                            Explore execution environment images
 9|- :inventory -i <inventory>          Explore an inventory
10|- :log                               Review the application log
11|- :lint <file or directory>          Lint Ansible/YAML files (experimental)
12|- :open                              Open current page in the editor
13|- :replay                            Explore a previous run using a playbook
artifact
14|- :run <playbook> -i <inventory>     Run a playbook in interactive mode
15|- :settings                          Review the current ansible-navigator
settings
16|- :quit                              Quit the application
17|
18|happy automating,
19|
20|-winston
```

The Welcome screen displays the options (in colon command format) that can be selected, and the list of options for navigating are at the bottom of the screen.

List the collections that are included within the Execution Environment image with the `:collections` option. The list of collections displayed will vary depending on the Execution Environment being used.

A number is displayed on the lefthand side of each collection. This value can be used to select and gain more insight into the details provided by the selected collection. To select a collection, type the colon (`:`) and the desired number. Various content types are displayed, depending on the collection that was selected.

To return to the previous page, press Esc. Continue to press Esc until you reach the page you want. This is particularly useful when you have navigated through multiple menus.

Configuring Automation Content Navigator

The default settings for Automation Content Navigator can be customized depending upon the desired use case. Individual settings can be specified as command-line arguments, environment variables, or within a settings file.

We have already seen some of the ways that settings can be provided as command-line arguments by specifying the `--eei` or `-m` flags. A configuration file can also be used to specify the settings that should be applied to Automation Content Navigator.

The file can be in either JSON or YAML format and and sourced from one of several locations:

./ansible-navigator.<ext>
: File within the current working directory

./ansible-navigator.<ext>
: Hidden file within the home directory of the current user

`ANSIBLE_NAVIGATOR_CONFIG`
: Environment variable specifying the path

The following is an snippet of a configuration file for Automation Content Navigator:

```
ansible-navigator:
  execution-environment:
    enabled: true
    container-engine: podman ❶
    pull:
      policy: missing ❷
  logging:
    level: warning
    append: true
    file: .ansible-navigator.log
  mode: stdout
  playbook-artifact: ❸
    enable: false
  time-zone: local
```

❶ Explicitly sets the container engine.

❷ Attempts to retrieve Execution Environment images from remote registries if not found locally.

❸ Playbook artifacts are files that contain details about every play and task.

Individual properties can also be defined using environment variables, and they are prefixed with `ANSIBLE_NAVIGATOR_`.

Running Playbooks

Aside from the other supporting features provided by Automation Content Navigator, its primary function is to run Ansible Playbooks. The unified method of running playbooks, all within an Execution Environment, ensures a consistent experience no matter where they operate.

The `ansible-navigator run` command is the entry point for running Ansible Playbooks. Most of the primitives that we have reviewed up to this point for running Ansible Playbooks still apply. However, there are important functional differences between running a standalone playbook using `ansible-playbook` and `ansible-navigator`:

Container-based execution

Since Automation Content Navigator leverages a container as its primary runtime, resources from the underlying host are mounted into the container. Only certain files and folders are bind-mounted from the host into the container. This impacts users that reference assets, like `vars_files`, from the host system during their automation. For most files and folders, only assets under the current working directory are available within the container. Additional volumes can be mounted by specifying the `--eev` flag using the format `--eev <volume_from_host>:<volume_in_container>:<options>`.

Environment variables defined on the host will also not be available, by default, within the container. The `--penv` flag can be used to specify the name of the environment variable that should be passed from the host into the container.

Both the `--eev` and `--penv` flags can be specified multiple times to enable adding multiple volumes and environment variables to the container used by Automation Content Navigator.

SSH

Ansible uses SSH as the primary method for connecting to remote hosts. Challenges may arise, depending upon the SSH configuration in use. SSH keys, located in nonstandard directories, can be mounted into the container using the `--eev` flag, as described previously. Support is available to automatically mount the default location for storing SSH keys for a user (`~/.ssh`).

However, it is recommended that the `ssh-agent`, an SSH key manager, be used as Automation Content Navigator has integration with this facility. Add SSH keys to `ssh-agent` using the `ssh-add` command, referencing the location of the SSH key.

Creating an example playbook

To demonstrate the use of Automation Content Navigator to execute playbooks, create a new playbook called *ansible-navigator-playbook.yml* with the following content:

```
- name: Playbook run within Automation Content Navigator
  hosts: localhost
  gather_facts: false
  vars:
    message: "Default Message"
  tasks:
    - name: Generate a random string
      ansible.builtin.set_fact:
        random_string: >-
          {{
```

```
        lookup(
          'community.general.random_string',
          min_lower=1,
          min_upper=1,
          min_special=1,
          min_numeric=1
        )
      }}

  - name: Print Random String
    ansible.builtin.debug:
      msg: "{{ random_string }}"

  - name: Print Message
    ansible.builtin.debug:
      msg: "{{ message }}"
```

Notice how the `community.general.random_string` lookup module is being used to generate a random string. Since this module and the `community.general` collection is not provided within the Ansible distribution, the Execution Environment (`ee-build`) created in the prior section can be leveraged; it includes the `community.general` collection.

Execute the following command to run the playbook created previously with `ansible-navigator` using the `ee-build` Execution Environment image also created previously:

```
ansible-navigator --pp=missing --eei localhost/ee-build:latest \
  -m stdout run ansible-content-navigator-playbook.yml
```

The `--pp=missing` flag sets the *pull policy* that instructs the container engine whether it should attempt to locate a more recent version of the Execution Environment image. Since the image was not published to a remote container registry, but is available locally, the `missing` option should be selected, which would only attempt to query the remote container registry if the image was not found locally.

Since Automation Content Navigator uses *interactive mode* as the default output, it offers the opportunity to explore the execution in finer detail. Notice how the list of plays from the playbook run is shown to provide a high-level overview of the state of the automation:

```
Play name                                            Ok  Changed  Unreachable
Failed  Skipped  Ignored  In progress  Task count  Progress
0│Playbook run within Automation Content Navigator  3   0         0
0       0        0        0            3           Complete
```

You can then investigate the individual actions that occurred within the play. Type `0` to explore the play and the tasks that were executed:

```
  Result  Host         Number  Changed  Task                       Task
  action              Duration
0|Ok      localhost    0       False    Generate a random string  ansible.
builtin.set_fact  0s
1|Ok      localhost    1       False    Print Random String       ansible.
builtin.debug     0s
2|Ok      localhost    2       False    Print Message             ansible.
builtin.debug     0s
```

Once you have finished exploring, type `:q` and press Enter to quit Automation Content Navigator.

To run the playbook in Automation Content Navigator where the output resembles how it appears when running `ansible-playbook`, add the `-m stdout` flag:

```
ansible-navigator --pp=missing --eei localhost/ee-build:latest \
  -m stdout run ansible-content-navigator-playbook.yml
```

Since the `ansible-navigator run` command allows the use of any of the flags provided by `ansible-playbook`, extra variables can be passed on the command line at runtime. The playbook created previously includes a variable called `message` with a default value of `message`. This value can be overridden at runtime using the `-e` flag. Set the value to `Automation Content Navigator is Awesome` using the following command:

```
ansible-navigator --pp=missing --eei localhost/ee-build:latest \
  -m stdout run ansible-navigator-playbook.yml \
  -e message="'Automation Content Navigator is Awesome'"
```

Notice in the `Print Message` task that the variable has been overridden successfully:

```
TASK [Print Message] ***********************************************************
ok: [localhost] => {
    "msg": "Automation Content Navigator is Awesome"
}
```

Conclusion

In this chapter, you explored how Execution Environments provide a consistent and reusable method of running automation. By creating an Execution Environment definition file, you learned how to construct an Execution Environment and use the `ansible-builder` utility to produce a container image. Finally, you investigated Automation Content Navigator as a unified way to run automation activities and how the tool leverages Execution Environments to perform Ansible automation.

In the next chapter, you will learn how Ansible plays a role in the management of systems.

CHAPTER 10

Managing Systems with Ansible

As we approach the conclusion of the book, we have seen several examples where you can apply Ansible automation—from deploying to a host, to configuring an application, to creating reusable components to make playbooks more maintainable.

Moreover, we also provided an introduction for how systems can be managed with Ansible, such as creating system users and groups, assigning permissions to files, and configuring the system.d daemon.

In this chapter, we will expand upon the infrastructure topic and focus on management-related tasks, including:

- Managing encryption keys
- Creating and configuring filesystems
- Task scheduling
- SELinux

Let's see how to manage encryption keys with Ansible.

Managing Keys

As discussed throughout this book, Ansible establishes an SSH connection to execute actions on a remote host. To establish this connectivity, authentication is accomplished using either a username/password combination or an SSH key pair. In this section, we'll focus on the keys.

SSH Authorization Keys

Let's see how SSH works when you authenticate from the control host to the remote host using SSH keys.

First, two asymmetric keys are required: one public key distributed to every host you need to communicate with (server in the case of SSH), and one private key stored in the control host (client), which you use to authenticate against the remote host. There are several ways to generate a a key pair, either using an Ansible user module, seen in previous chapters, or the `ssh-keygen` tool.

Before we look at how to manage these keys with Ansible, let's explore how SSH key-based authentication works.

SSH Key-Based Authentication

As mentioned, this authentication method requires two keys associated with a user: one private key and one public key. Public key content must be distributed to each remote host in a file named *authorized_keys* and stored in the *<user_home>/.ssh* directory.

When the client wants to access a remote host through the SSH protocol, the following occurs (see Figure 10-1):

1. The client establishes a connection to the server part with a concrete user.
2. The server sends a random plain message to the client.
3. The client uses the private key to encrypt the message and return it to the server.
4. The server decrypts the message with the public key stored at *<user_home>/.ssh/authorized_keys*. Access is granted if the message is sent the first time to the client. Otherwise, access is denied.

With an understanding of how SSH key-based authentication method works, let's see how Ansible automates the distribution of the keys.

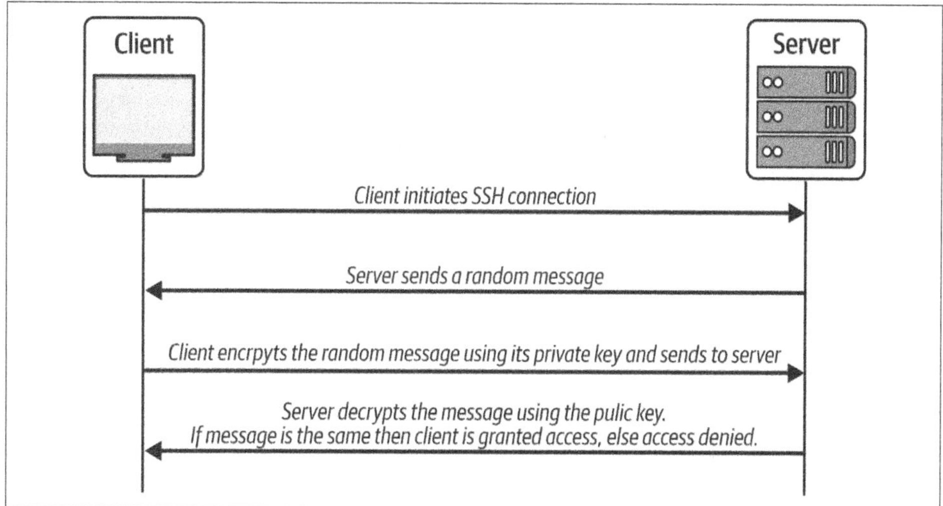

Figure 10-1. SSH key based authentication

Authorized Key Module

Ansible includes the `ansible.posix.authorized_key` module to manage the SSH public key associated with the authorized key file. This module has two key parameters: the `user` parameter represents the username on the remote host whose *authorized_keys* file will be created or modified. The `key` parameter represents the SSH public key content as a string or the URL where the key is stored.

You can use the `lookup` plug-in to access the content stored in a file from the control host.

Let's develop a playbook that creates and copies the public keys of two users to each of the hosts defined in the inventory file. For this example, we'll use the `vars_files` property to define the details sourced from a JSON file instead of hardcoding the content directly within the playbook.

Create a new file named *users.json* with the following content:

```
users: ❶
  - {username: 'Ada',
     password: '$y$j9T$68mjAbPmPM.0veTrWjXNx.$FdvdDAE92QRWE/L2p.
     mcMjB3gOqEu0Ki3rPtZvxLCLC',
     keyfile: './id_rsa_ada.pub' } ❷
  - {username: 'Alexandra',
    password: '$y$j9T$68mjAbPmPM.0veTrWjXNx.$FdvdDAE92QRWE/L2p.
```

```
        mcMjB3gOqEu0Ki3rPtZvxLCLC',
        keyfile: './id_rsa_aixa.pub' }
```

❶ Variable name containing the list of elements

❷ Each element of the list

The playbook will iterate over all of the elements in the file, create each user, and copy the public key to all defined hosts:

```
---
- hosts: all
  become: yes
  vars_files:
    - users.json ❶
  tasks:
    - name: create users
      ansible.builtin.user:
        name: "{{ item.username }}" ❷
        password: "{{ item.password }}"
        shell: /bin/bash
        state: present
      loop: "{{ users }}" ❸

    - name: upload ssh public key to users authorized keys file
      ansible.builtin.authorized_key: ❹
        user: '{{ item.username }}' ❺
        state: present ❻
        manage_dir: yes ❼
        key: "{{ lookup('file', './{{ item.keyfile }}') }}" ❽
      loop: "{{ users }}"
```

❶ File with users

❷ Sets the name of the user from the `username` value

❸ Iterates over all elements defined in the `users` field

❹ Uses the `authorized_key` module to copy the public key to the remote host

❺ Associates the user to store the public key

❻ If set to `absent`, removes the public key

❼ The module will create the directory, as well as set the owner and permissions of an existing directory

❽ Copies the public key from the local path to the remote host

When executing this playbook, you enable the SSH key authentication process for all hosts defined in the inventory file with the users defined in the JSON file. Another important process when managing systems with Ansible is configuring disks and filesystems. We will elaborate on the various processes in the following section.

Managing Disks

Another typical task that is performed by infrastructure administrators is managing disk systems. These tasks include creating partitions, creating filesystems, mounting, and managing logical volumes (LVs).

In this section, we will explore and execute some of these tasks using Ansible. The Ansible ecosystem provides different modules for managing disks. For example, the `community.general.filesystem` module uses, among other tools, `blkid`, `mkfs`, or `e2fsprogs`, while the `community.general.parted` module uses the `parted` command-line tool.

Let's look at some of the Ansible modules that are used to manage filesystems.

Managing a Filesystem with the filesystem Module

Using the `community.general.filesystem` module, let's create a filesystem. This module has some requirements for the target host to execute:

- It uses specific tools related to the `fstype` to create or resize a filesystem (from packages including `e2fsprogs`, `xfsprogs`, `dosfstools`, etc.). Depending on the filesystem, install the appropriate tool to use.
- It uses generic tools, mostly related to the OS, such as `blkid` or `mkfs`.
- On FreeBSD, either the `util-linux` or `e2fsprogs` package is required.

There are two important parameters to set when using this module. The first is `dev`, which targets paths to block devices in Linux, character devices in FreeBSD, or as a regular file. The second is `fstype`, which is used to create the filesystem type (i.e., `ext3`, `ext4`, `lvm`, ...).

To create an `ext4` filesystem on a device:

```
- name: Create a ext4 filesystem
  community.general.filesystem:
    fstype: ext4 ❶
    dev: /dev/sdb1 ❷
```

❶ Sets the filesystem type

❷ The device to format

You can rewrite the same example by setting the parameters to the `mkfs` command using the `opts` parameter:

```
- name: Create a ext4 filesystem and check disk blocks
  community.general.filesystem:
    fstype: ext4
    dev: /dev/sdb1
    opts: -cc ❶
```

❶ Sets the check disk blocks option to the `mkfs` invocation

As with most modules in Ansible, the `state` parameter is also supported to wipe out a partition:

```
- name: Blank filesystem signature
  community.general.filesystem:
    dev: /dev/sdb1
    state: absent
```

You can also mount a filesystem into a file by setting the `dev` parameter referencing the file:

```
- name: Create a filesystem on top of a regular file
  community.general.filesystem:
    dev: ./disk.img
    fstype: vfat
```

Apart from the parameters shown in these examples, this module also permits the following parameters:

`force`
: A Boolean parameter that allows the creation of a new filesystem on devices that already have a filesystem.

`fstype`
: Type of filesystem that will be created. The possible values for this parameter are: `bcachefs`, `btrfs`, `ext2`, `ext3`, `ext4`, `ext4dev`, `f2fs`, `lvm`, `ocfs2`, `reiserfs`, `xfs`, `vfat`, `swap`, and `ufs`.

`resizefs`
: A Boolean parameter to set if the block device and filesystem size differ, and if so, grow the filesystem into the space.

`uuid`
: This sets the UUID of the filesystem to the given value.

With an understanding of how to create a filesystem on a device, let's see an example of how to mount a device.

Mounting a Device

The `ansible.posix.mount` module controls active and configured mount points in the */etc/fstab* file. The *fstab* file contains a list of all available partitions (disk or not); it is read by the `mount` command to ensure correct mounting behavior.

To mount a volume, set the `path` property to the location where to mount the volume, the device to mount, and the filesystem type. The final step is to set the `state` property to `mounted`.

The following example mounts the device `/dev/sample` to the path `/data1`:

```
- name: mount the device on /data1
  ansible.posix.mount:
    path: /data1
    src: /dev/sample
    fstype: xfs
    state: mounted
```

To unmount a device, set the `state` to `unmounted`:

```
- name: Unmount a mounted volume
  ansible.posix.mount:
    path: /tmp/mnt-pnt
    state: unmounted
```

The `src` parameter can be a network filesystem like NFS or Samba. The following example shows how to use the `mount` module to access an NFS volume:

```
- name: Mount an NFS volume
  ansible.posix.mount:
    src: 192.168.1.100:/nfs/ssd/shared_data
    path: /mnt/shared_data
    opts: rw,sync,hard
    state: mounted
    fstype: nfs
```

There are many different valid values for the `state` parameter that change how the module behaves. Let's explore the options:

`mounted`
: The device will be actively mounted and appropriately configured within the *fstab* file. If the mount point is not present, it will be created.

`unmounted`
: The device will be unmounted without changing the *fstab* file.

`present`
: Only specifies that the device is to be configured in the *fstab* file and does not trigger or require a mount.

`ephemeral`
: Only specifies that the device is to be mounted without changing the *fstab* file. If it is already mounted, a remount will be triggered. If the mount point path already has a device mounted on it, and its source is different than `src`, the module will fail to avoid an unexpected unmount or mount point override. If the mount point is not present, it will be created.

`absent`
: Specifies that the mount point entry path will be removed from the *fstab* file and will also unmount the mounted device and remove the mount point. A mounted device will be unmounted regardless of the `src` property or its real source. `absent` does not unmount recursively, and the module will fail if multiple devices are mounted on the same mount point. Using `absent` with a mount point that is not registered in the *fstab* file has no effect. Use the `unmounted` value instead.

`remounted`
: Specifies that the device will be remounted when you want to force a refresh on the mount itself.

`absent_from_fstab`
: Specifies that the mount entry for the device will be removed from the *fstab* file. This option does not unmount or delete the mount point.

Next, we will discuss the `parted` module.

Managing a Filesystem with the parted Module

This module allows configuring block device partitions using the `parted` command-line tool. This module requires the `parted` tool to be installed in the remote host.

Let's review some examples using the `parted` module:

```
- name: Create a new ext3 primary partition
  community.general.parted:
    device: /dev/sdb
    number: 1 ❶
    state: present
    fs_type: ext3

- name: Remove partition number 1
  community.general.parted:
    device: /dev/sdb
    number: 1
    state: absent

- name: Create a new primary partition with a size of 10GiB
  community.general.parted:
```

```
    device: /dev/sdb
    number: 1
    state: present
    part_end: 10GiB ❷

- name: Create a new primary partition with a size of 5GiB at disk's end
  community.general.parted:
    device: /dev/sdb
    number: 3
    state: present
    fs_type: ext3
    part_start: -5GiB ❸

- name: Read device information (always use unit when probing)
  community.general.parted: device=/dev/sdb unit=MiB
  register: sdb_info ❹
```

❶ Sets the partition number.

❷ Sets where the partition will end as an offset from the beginning of the disk. The offset can be an absolute number (5 GB) or relative (70%) values.

❸ Where the partition will start as an offset from the beginning of the disk. The offset can be absolute or relative values.

❹ Stores the response related to the partition within this variable.

Thus far, standard partitions have been explored. In the following section, we will introduce you to Logical Volume Management (LVM) and LVs.

Logical Volume Management

You cannot extend or reduce the primary partition, which can cause issues when additional disk space is needed. However, this limitation can be avoided with Logical Volume Management as it allows you to add or remove disks within a logical volume. LVM provides an abstraction layer over physical storage, enabling the creation of logical storage volumes. This approach offers greater flexibility than using physical storage directly.

LVM has the following components:

Physical volume (PV)
: A partition or whole disk designated for LVM use.

Volume group (VG)
: A collection of physical volumes that forms a pool of disk space, allowing you to allocate logical volumes.

Logical volume (LV)
: Represents a usable storage device.

Figure 10-2 illustrates the components of LVM.

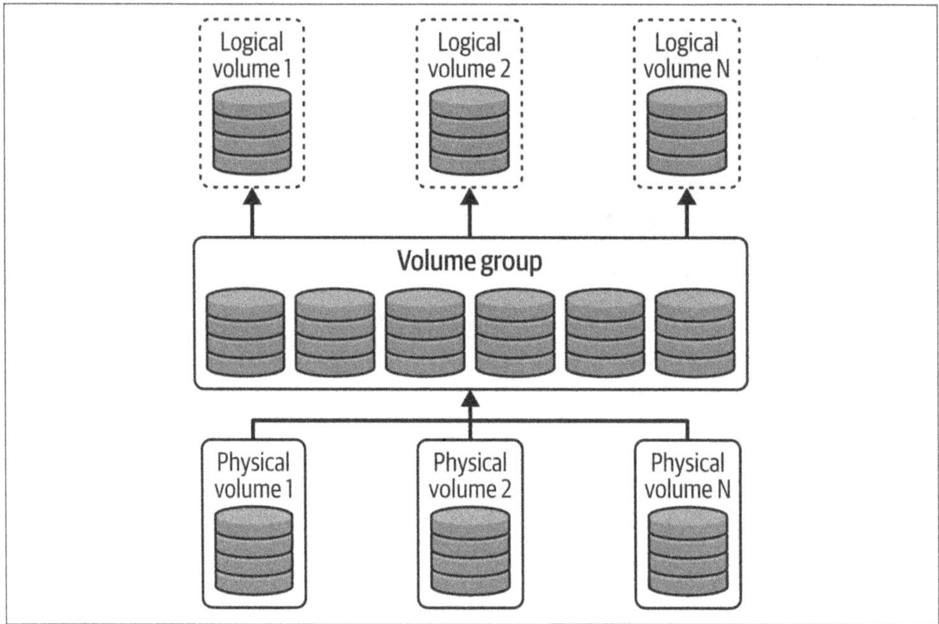

Figure 10-2. LVM logical volume components

Before beginning a discussion about LVM, it is important to note that the `lvm2` package needs to be installed on the remote hosts where you want to create and manage the logical volumes.

To work with LVMs and Ansible, several modules are available:

`parted`
: Creates the partition. The `lvm` flag must be configured to enable the capability.

`lvg`
: Creates the volume group.

`lvol`
: Creates the logical volume belonging to the created volume group.

`filesystem`
: Formats the logical volume to the desired filesystem.

`mount`
: The module optionally mounts the logical volume.

Let's see a playbook that executes all the previous steps, creating a single volume group containing a logical volume:

```
- name: LVM 2 GB partition
  hosts: all
  become: true
  tasks:
    - name: create partition
      community.general.parted:
        device: /dev/sdb
        number: 1
        flags: [ lvm ] ❶
        state: present
        part_end: 2GB
    - name: task for creating volume group
      community.general.lvg:
          vg: sample-vg ❷
          pvs: /dev/sdb ❸
          pesize: 16M ❹
    - name: task for creating logical volume
      community.general.lvol:
          vg: sample-vg ❺
          lv:  sample-lv ❻
          size: 2g
          force: yes
    - name: format the xfs filesystem
      community.general.filesystem:
        fstype: xfs
        dev: /dev/sample-vg/sample-lv ❼

    - name: mount the lv on /data1
      community.general.mount:
        path: /data1
        src: /dev/sample-vg/sample-lv
        fstype: xfs
        state: mounted
```

❶ Creates a new primary partition for LVM

❷ Volume group name

❸ List of comma-separated devices to use as physical devices in this volume group

❹ Physical extent size

❺ The volume group this logical volume belongs to

❻ Logical volume name

❼ Formats the logical volume using the name of the group

In this section, you learned basic disk management operations, from standard partitions to LVMs, and how they can be managed with Ansible. Next, you will learn another important topic when managing systems: scheduling `cron` jobs.

Scheduling Tasks with cron Jobs

It is essential for system administrators to automate as many tasks as possible, especially when they need to run at a specific time or at a certain time period. Examples include creating a backup, sending logs, or removing temporary files.

In Linux, we have the `cron` tool, a time-based job scheduler that automates the execution of scripts and commands at specified intervals or times. `cron` is composed of two elements:

cron Daemon `crond`
: This background service runs continuously, checking for any scheduled tasks that need to be executed. The daemon wakes up periodically to check for tasks in the `cron` tables.

crontab `Cron Table`
: This is where you define the scheduled jobs in the *crontab* file.

The `ansible.builtin.cron` module is provided by Ansible for the purpose of managing *crontab* files. The following example demonstrates how to add a new `cron` entry to the *crontab* file to execute an `ls` command every 2 minutes. The command to execute is specified within the `job` parameter:

```
- hosts: all
  tasks:
    - name: Create a cron job
      ansible.builtin.cron:
        name: list_files
        minute: "*/2" ❶
        job: "ls > /dev/null"
```

❶ Minute when the job should be run (in this case, every 2 minutes)

In the previous example, you configured a `cron` job to run the `job` command every 2 minutes. Let's create a `cron` job that executes every day at 23:59:

```
- hosts: all
  tasks:
    - name: Create a cron job
      ansible.builtin.cron:
```

```
        name: do_backup
        hour: "23" ❶
        minute: "59" ❷
        job: "do-backup.sh"
```

❶ Sets the specific hour when the job should be executed

❷ Sets the specific minute when the job should be executed

Apart from setting hours and minutes, Ansible allows you to set the following time units: `month`, `weekday`, and `day`. The default value is `*`, meaning there is no restriction on that time unit.

Use the `user` parameter to set the specific user whose *crontab* file should be modified. It defaults to the current user.

You can use the `state` parameter with the `absent` value to remove a `cron` entry:

```
- hosts: all
  tasks:
    - name: Removes a cron job
      ansible.builtin.cron:
        name: list_files
        state: absent
```

`cron` jobs let you easily schedule the execution of commands, automating certain tasks that every system administrator should run periodically.

Before finishing this chapter, we'll explore the topic of managing security, particularly when configuring and managing SELinux or SSH access.

Managing Security

The last part of this chapter covers how to manage security elements when using Ansible. These can include SELinux configuration, SSH configuration, and registering repositories securely.

Let's review how to configure the SSH service.

SSH Configuration

At the beginning of the chapter, you saw how to share keys with remote hosts to permit key authentication instead of using a username and password. Apart from generating and distributing the keys, you might also configure the SSH server with specific parameters.

SSH offers a number of configuration parameters that can be specified in the */etc/ssh/sshd_config* file. For example, one of these parameters is the `MaxAuthTries` setting, which limits the number of authentication attempts a user can make. Setting this property is essential as it can avoid a brute force attack. By default, in the *sshd_config* file, the parameter is commented out (not enabled) and is defined as:

```
# Authentication:

#LoginGraceTime 2m
#PermitRootLogin prohibit-password
#StrictModes yes
#MaxAuthTries 6
#MaxSessions 10

#PubkeyAuthentication yes
```

A good practice is to enable the `MaxAuthTries` property and set it to a lower value. For this task, you can use the `lineinfile` module to replace one value with another:

```
- name: SSH configuration
  hosts: all
  become: true
  tasks:
    - name: Replace MaxAuthTries
      ansible.builtin.lineinfile: ❶
        path: /etc/ssh/sshd_config
        regexp: "^#MaxAuthTries " ❷
        line: "MaxAuthTries 3" ❸
      notify: Restart ssh ❹
  handlers:
    - name: Restart ssh
      ansible.builtin.service:
        name: sshd
        state: restarted
```

❶ Specifies the use of the `lineinfile` module

❷ Locates the commented parameter in the file

❸ Specifies `MaxAuthTries 3` as the value to apply

❹ Restarts the SSH service so changes take effect (when a change occurs)

This is just one example. The same approach can be used for any other configuration parameter, either from the SSH service or another service.

Since Ansible uses SSH for transport, take care with configuring the sshd on the remote node as you might misconfigure and be unable to reach the remote host!

The next section describes how to register new repositories within systems (in this case, yum repositories) by enabling a GNU Privacy Guard check.

YUM Repositories

To register a yum repository and validate its GNU Privacy Guard (GPG) key, two modules are needed. The first is rpm_key, which adds (or removes) a GPG key to the RPM database. Second is yum_repository, which allows for the addition (or removal) of YUM repositories in an RPM-based Linux distribution.

Let's see an example that adds the MySQL 8.4 Community Server YUM repository to the system and enables GPG checking:

```
- name: Registers YUM repository
  hosts: database
  become: true
  tasks:
    - name: import GPG key
      ansible.builtin.rpm_key:
        state: present
        key: https://repo.mysql.com/RPM-GPG-KEY-mysql ❶
    - name: Add repository configuration entries
      ansible.builtin.yum_repository:
        name: mysql84-community
        description: MySQL YUM repo
        baseurl: https://repo.mysql.com/yum/mysql-8.4-community/el/8/$basearch ❷
        gpgcheck: true ❸
        gpgkey: https://repo.mysql.com/RPM-GPG-KEY-mysql ❹
        enabled: true
```

❶ Key to import

❷ YUM repository URL

❸ Specifies whether YUM should or should not perform a GPG signature when checking packages

❹ A URL referencing the GPG key file for the repository

GPG checking is important in order to validate that the packages YUM installs originate from a trusted repository instead of one that could potentially install malware or any other malicious software. You can add the GPG key file into the Ansible playbook so the checking doesn't depend on an external site that could also be compromised.

The final section of this chapter focuses on configuring SELinux.

SELinux

Security-Enhanced Linux (SELinux) is a security architecture integrated into the Linux kernel that provides mandatory access control. It enforces fine-grained security policies on system resources, enhancing the operating system's overall security.

You will use the `linux-system-roles.selinux` Ansible role (*https://oreil.ly/z-qCH*) to configure SELinux within managed nodes. This role provides the following features:

- Set enforcing/permissive states
- Perform restorecon on directories of the filesystem tree
- Set/get Booleans
- Set/get file contexts
- Manage logins
- Manage ports

It is important to note that everything in this role is based on setting Ansible variables; no module is explicitly invoked. For example, to modify the SELinux port mapping, create a variable named `selinux_ports` with a list of all mapping ports:

```
selinux_ports:
  - ports: <port_number> ❶
    proto: tcp
    setype: http_port_t ❷
    state: present
```

❶ Sets the port number to which you want to assign the `http_port_t` SELinux type

❷ The SELinux type of the SELinux port definition

Installing the role

To install `linux-system-roles.selinux` in control node, use the `ansible-galaxy` utility:

```
ansible-galaxy role install linux-system-roles.selinux
```

Moreover, this role requires that `ansible.posix` and `community.general` collections be installed as well:

```
ansible-galaxy collection install ansible.posix
ansible-galaxy collection install community.general
```

With the requirements installed, let's use this Ansible role to configure SELinux.

Examples

For the first example, you will see how to set the SELinux state to `enforcing`, and map port 22100 to to the `ssh_port_t` SELinux port type:

```
- name: Manage SELinux policy example
  hosts: all
  become: true
  vars:
    selinux_state: enforcing ❶
    selinux_ports:
      - { ports:"22100", proto:"tcp", setype:"ssh_port_t", state:"present" } ❷
  tasks:
    - name: Run SELinux role ❸
      ansible.builtin.include_role:
        name: linux-system-roles.selinux
  post_tasks:
    - name: Reboot the systems ❹
      ansible.builtin.reboot:
```

❶ Sets `enforcing` mode

❷ Uses JSON form to set the parameters

❸ Executes the role with variables set

❹ Reboots the machine so changes take effect

SELinux Boolean values determine whether a specific policy should be enforced or not. For example, the `httpd_can_network_connect` Boolean controls whether the Apache web server can make network connections. To enable this, the `selinux_booleans` variable should be added:

```
- name: Manage SELinux policy example
  hosts: all
  become: true
  vars:
    selinux_state: enforcing
    selinux_policy: targeted ❶
    selinux_booleans:
      - name: httpd_can_network_connect ❷
        state: true
        persistent: true ❸
...
```

❶ Uses the `targeted` SELinux policy type

❷ Sets the control to *on*

❸ Sets the change permanently

SELinux controls the contexts to determine which users, applications, and services can access which files, directories, and applications. This prevents users or applications from accessing directories or files out of their scope. To set this mapping with Ansible, use the `selinux_fcontexts` variable.

Suppose the `httpd` service exposes a web page located in the */webpage* directory. Let's make it so that the `httpd` process can only access this directory:

```
selinux_fcontexts:
  - target: '/webpage(/.*)?'
    setype: 'httpd_sys_content_t'
    state: present
```

An SELinux user is an identifier that administrators use to restrict which SELinux roles are accessible. Each Linux account is mapped to precisely one SELinux user, while an SELinux user can be associated with multiple roles.

To manage SELinux users, the `selinux_logins` variable can be used. Let's map the `alex` Linux user to the `staff_u` SELinux user:

```
selinux_logins:
  - login: alex
    seuser: staff_u
    serange: s0-s0:c0.c1023 ❶
    state: present
```

❶ Sets the SELinux MLS range for the user

It is also possible to manage SELinux modules using `selinux_modules` variables:

```
selinux_modules:
  - path: localpolicy.cil ❶
    priority: 300
    state: enabled
  - name: unconfineduser ❷
    priority: 100
    state: disabled
  - name: temporarypolicy ❸
    priority: 400
    state: absent
```

❶ Installs the `localpolicy.cil` module with priority 300

❷ Disables the `unconfineduser` module with priority 100

❸ Removes the `temporarypolicy` module with priority 400

Conclusion

In this chapter, you saw how to manage systems using Ansible. We showed you how to do tasks such as distributing SSH keys, formatting devices, and configuring SELinux.

When you started this book, you may have only had a little knowledge about Ansible. Now, you not only have a good understanding of the Ansible project, but when to use it, how to automate day-to-day tasks such as updating servers, and how to roll update applications safely. You are now ready to become an Ansible certified engineer and get a boost in your career.

Index

Symbols

A

D

E

F

G

H

I

J

O

P

Q

R

S

T

U

About the Authors

Alex Soto Bueno is a director of developer experience at Red Hat. He is passionate about the Java world and software automation, and he believes in the open source software model. He has done numerous Ansible Deep Dives as part of the Red Hat DevNation efforts. Alex is the coauthor of the *GitOps Cookbook* (O'Reilly), *Testing Java Microservices* (Manning), *Quarkus Cookbook* (O'Reilly), and *Kubernetes Secrets Management* (Manning), and a contributor to several open source projects. A Java Champion since 2017, he is also an international speaker and teacher at Salle URL University.

Andrew Block is a distinguished architect at Red Hat who works with organizations to design and implement solutions leveraging cloud native technologies. He specializes in continuous integration and continuous delivery methodologies to reduce delivery time and automate how environments are built and maintained. Andrew is the author of several publications on solutions within the Kubernetes ecosystem, a maintainer on the Helm project, and a contributor to several open source projects, including sigstore, which provides tooling for securing the software delivery process.

Colophon

The animal on the cover of *Red Hat Certified Engineer (RHCE) Ansible Automation Study Guide* is a Raggiana bird-of-paradise (*Paradisaea raggiana*), the national bird of Papua New Guinea, which can be found living in the foothills and forest edges of the country.

The Raggiana bird-of-paradise is relatively large, measuring 13 inches long, on average. It is sexually dimorphic. The male Raggiana bird-of-paradise has a yellow cowl, green throat, and red and orange tail feathers. Both males and females have yellow eyes, black breasts, and overall maroon-brown coloring. They eat fruit and arthropods.

The Raggiana bird-of-paradise has a decreasing population and a conservation status of Least Concern with the IUCN Red List of Threatened Species. Many of the animals on O'Reilly covers are endangered; all of them are important to the world.

The cover illustration is by José Marzan Jr., based on an antique line engraving from *Wood's Animate Creations*. The series design is by Edie Freedman, Ellie Volckhausen, and Karen Montgomery. The cover fonts are Gilroy Semibold and Guardian Sans. The text font is Adobe Minion Pro; the heading font is Adobe Myriad Condensed; and the code font is Dalton Maag's Ubuntu Mono.

www.ingramcontent.com/pod-product-compliance
Lightning Source LLC
Chambersburg PA
CBHW061419210326
41598CB00035B/6268

9781098162139